Architectural and
Ornament Drawings

Architectural and Ornament Drawings:

JUVARRA, VANVITELLI,

THE BIBIENA FAMILY, & OTHER

ITALIAN DRAUGHTSMEN

Catalogue by Mary L. Myers

Associate Curator, Department of Prints and Photographs

The Metropolitan Museum of Art

1975

Copyright © 1975 by The Metropolitan Museum of Art

Design by Peter Oldenburg

Composition by Finn Typographic Service

Printing by The Leether Press

LIBRARY OF CONGRESS CATALOGING IN PUBLICATION DATA

Myers, Mary L.
    Architectural and ornament drawings.

    1. Drawings, Italian — Exhibitions. 2. Decoration and ornament,
Architectural — Italy. 3. Decoration and ornament, Italian. 4. Art-
ists' preparatory studies — Italy. I. New York (City). Metropolitan
Museum of Art. II. Title.

NC255.M9   741.9'45   74-32459

ISBN 0-87099-126-4

Foreword

From about 1900 to 1960 American museums collected at the fastest rate and with the widest interests that the world has ever seen. This sweepstake ingurgitation has now pumped the sources dry and has sent prices skyrocketing for what remains, just at a time when American museum funds are falling behind the rate of general inflation. But the result is not entirely disastrous, for it forces us to take stock of what we raked together bit by bit as chances offered, and to catalogue the holdings that have grown almost without our being aware of the growth. While a few excellent catalogues have been published, mostly by the Morgan Library, the Frick Collection, and this Museum, American collections are still so little known that we ourselves in the museums are unaware of treasures in nearby museums, and are sometimes unaware of remarkable things in other departments of our very own buildings. It would be useful if all American museums would pool their resources for countrywide surveys of some scarcer specialities like, say, German drawings, Islamic glass, Greek jewelry, or Romanesque sculpture.

In this catalogue Mary L. Myers publishes a selection of the Metropolitan Museum's drawings for stage sets, furniture, silver, architecture, and many other forms of applied art. To show these practical drawings in use, she has selected many that are projects for known works of art. Yet however utilitarian in intention, these drawings often achieve the perfection that is sometimes attainable in the decorative arts, but never in the more complex overtones of the expressive arts.

A. Hyatt Mayor
Curator Emeritus, Prints

5

Introduction

It is often a surprise to visitors to the Museum's Print Study Room that we possess, as a complement to our collection of architectural and ornament prints and books, a large collection of architectural and ornament drawings. William M. Ivins, Jr., the first curator of the Department of Prints, founded in 1917, set about building a comprehensive collection of printed architecture and ornament as a natural addition to our collection of engravings, etchings, and lithographs. His essays on the ornament collection and on the many exhibitions of ornament he arranged show that he felt that an engraving of a metalwork design by a master silversmith was as telling for its period as a fresco or etching.

It may be useful to explain here why two of the Museum's departments contain drawings: the Department of Drawings and the Department of Prints and Photographs. The Department of Drawings was created only in 1960. Before that time figure drawings were not acquired in the systematic fashion that their specialized department acquires them now; instead, they were collected by the Curator of European Paintings as significant works came to his attention. Through the forty-three years preceding the founding of the Department of Drawings, ornament prints and drawings were added to the collection in the Print Room. By 1960 that collection was an impressive one, and the maintenance of its unity seemed in the long run more useful than breaking it up and adding architectural and ornament drawings to the figure drawings in the Drawings Department.

The first major purchase of architectural and ornament drawings was in 1934, when William Ivins bought a large scrapbook of English drawings containing designs by Robert and James Adam, William Chambers, James Wyatt, and Thomas Hardwick. When A. Hyatt Mayor became curator in 1946 he began to buy ornament drawings whenever he found them. In 1949, we received our first considerable group of Italian ornament drawings when we acquired part of Janos Scholz's collection of drawings for ornament and book illustration. Although that lot contained several Italian eighteenth-century drawings, it was composed primarily of sixteenth-century drawings. In 1952, the bulk of Janos Scholz's ornament drawings came to us, and within the lot was a series of eighteenth-century drawings that formed the nucleus of the collection that has expanded regularly since. Among the Scholz drawings were most of our Bolognese drawings, including those in the exhibition by Carlo Bianconi (Nos. 5–7), Flaminio Minozzi (Nos. 44 a and b), and Mauro Tesi (Nos. 57, 58), as well as an extraordinary group of drawings by Giovanni Battista Foggini (Nos. 23, 24, 26), more extensive than any I know outside of Florence and Rome.

Within the last decade, our collection of eighteenth-century Italian drawings has grown into one of the important collections of its kind. In 1964, seven drawings after Luigi Vanvitelli's theater at Caserta and the festivities he designed to honor the marriage of Ferdinando, king of Naples and Maria Carolina of Austria were purchased (Nos. 69–75). This acquisition inspired the generous gift of Donald Oenslager's collection of five drawings by Vanvitelli (Nos. 62, 64–67). With the subsequent purchase of three others, the Museum's collection of Vanvitelli drawings became the most comprehensive known outside those in Naples and Caserta. A large scrapbook of Piedmontese drawings comprising designs for church and palace interiors, altars, fountains, stage sets, and other decorations, was given to the Museum in 1965 by Leon Dalva (Nos. 30, 40–43, 81). These drawings give a broad and clear idea of design in that region that served as a fertile ground for ideas passing back and forth from Italy to France, Austria, and Germany. In 1969, John McKendry, who succeeded A. Hyatt Mayor as curator, purchased for the department a volume of drawings by Filippo Juvarra (No. 36). One of the five Juvarra albums outside of Italy, it is the only one in the United States. Two years later the purchase of a number of drawings from the collection of Sidney Kaufman of London added several important sheets by, among others, members of the Bibiena family, two of which are exhibited here (Nos. 9, 10), stage sets by Mauro Berti (No. 3), Serafino Brizzi (No. 19), Fabrizio and Bernardino Galliari (No. 31), a sheet by Vanvitelli (No. 68), and an interesting group of anonymous drawings (Nos. 80, 83, 84). Seventy-two formerly unknown drawings, most of them preparations for engravings of projects of different members of the Bibiena family, were purchased in 1972 (Nos.

11–17). Finally, as this catalogue was being written, we acquired, with the assistance of the Ian Woodner Family Foundation, a group of drawings by Giovanni Battista Natali, a draughtsman whose works have often been attributed to better-known artists, such as Ferdinando Bibiena (Nos. 48–51).

New York has rich collections of architectural and ornament material. Columbia University's Avery Library is one of the world's great architectural libraries. The combination of the collections of ornament and architectural drawings of the Metropolitan Museum's Department of Prints and Photographs and that of the Department of Prints and Drawings at the Cooper-Hewitt Museum (formerly the Cooper Union Museum), as A. Hyatt Mayor has observed, now makes New York *the* place to study ornament, along with Berlin. The older, comprehensive collection of ornament in the Ornamentstichsammlung in the Kunstbibliothek there, despite its losses in World War II, remains the major European center for studying ornament.

The person who prepared the ground for the study of New York's collections of ornament drawings was Rudolf Berliner. He catalogued the twelve thousand from the Piancastelli collection (see Lugt S 2078a and 1860c) acquired by the Cooper-Hewitt Museum. That was a herculean task to which he applied his profound knowledge of European decorative arts and drawings. He also made many visits to the Metropolitan Museum's Print Room. I well remember in the early sixties a gentle, modest man who freely identified and discussed our drawings with Hyatt Mayor and Janet Byrne. He never wrote his observations on the mats as many scholars do—they appear always in the hand of one of our staff members—and as his time was always short, and he had much material to work through, the notes were brief and not attributed to him. I cannot emphasize enough, however, the enormous debt that this catalogue owes to him. He prepared the foundation for the study of our collection just as he had done with Cooper-Hewitt's. My debt to Rudolf Berliner is, in fact, a dual one; I studied the collection at Cooper-Hewitt at every turn, and it was often a drawing there that he had catalogued that identified one of ours. His contributions were pervasive but nearly anonymous, and I have not always been able to give the specific credit due him in the individual entries.

The aim of this exhibition is to present as comprehensive a view of eighteenth-century Italian ornament and architectural draughtsmanship as our collection allows. One name is conspicuously absent—that of Giovanni Battista Piranesi, who designed the small church of S. Maria del Priorato on the Aventine hill in Rome and was charged with some work for the interior of the Lateran. However, Piranesi is well represented in other New York collections: the Pierpont Morgan Library possesses drawings for S. Maria del Priorato and the Avery Library, projects for the Lateran.

Although this exhibition focuses on the eighteenth century, the limits are not strict. The sheet by Juvarra's master, Carlo Fontana (No. 29), the most influential and active architect in Rome at the beginning of the century, was included, although our drawing is an early one, dating to the 1660s. The situation is the same for the end of the century; although the projects in our drawings by Felice Giani (No. 33) are not precisely identified or dated, they may well have been made in the second decade of the nineteenth century. However, Giani's neoclassic outlook was formed in the eighteenth century, and thus presents a fitting conclusion to the evolution of ornament styles shown in the exhibition.

The projects presented in this selection of drawings are diverse. Furniture design is represented by sketches for an armchair, a table, and a mirror frame. Metalwork is represented by designs for clocks, coffee urns, and ecclesiastical objects. There are even designs for calling cards.

There are designs for interior decoration: projects for ceiling and wall painting and stucco work, and even a sketch of a bed alcove. The painted walls and ceilings of Italian palaces during this period were often decorated with illusionistic perspective views in an architectural setting. This feigned, painted architecture is known as *quadratura,* and its painter, a *quadraturista.* Pictures, often inserted into the *quadratura* as if distinctly framed, independent paintings, are called *quadri riportati.* They were often, in the eighteenth century, views, or *vedute,* but were sometimes figural. For example, the scenes of the Passion in Vincenzo dal Rè's ceiling (No. 54), are *quadri riportati* in a *quadratura* background. *Quadratura* was also often combined with stucco so that sham architecture had, in fact, some three-dimensionality. Some of the curling foliage in the dal Rè ceiling, thus, may have been intended for execution in stucco.

Designers often prepared their inventions for the engraver. Many of our drawings of cartouches were probably meant to be engraved in pattern books as models for other craftsmen and students. Engravings were also made in honor of a prince or other patron; the Bibiena catafalque designs (Nos. 15–17) are drawings for prints to honor the deceased. Likewise, the engravings that were projected after the drawings for Francesco Bibiena's Nancy theater (Nos. 11–12) would have glorified Leopold, duke of Lorraine, who had commissioned the theater.

Stage designs, which may be considered the Italian eighteenth century's ultimate expression of architecture and ornament in combination, are presented in great number. Also represented is another aspect of eighteenth-century theater, the *Theatra Sacra,* designs for church celebrations, executed, for instance, for those held during Holy Week.

Another form of temporary religious decoration represented here is for the celebration of the canonization of a saint (No. 38). There are also a number of catafalques, allied by virtue of their temporary nature to designs for fêtes and the stage.

A number of the drawings in this catalogue are described as having a Gothic *A* stamped in purple ink either on the drawing or on its mount. This Gothic *A* was described by Lugt (Lugt S 47a) as an unidentified mark on a collection of drawings which, he reported, may have belonged to the Savoia-Aosta family and was said to have been found in a family palace in Brianza, the region between Milan and Lake Como. Rudolf Berliner thought it strange, if not impossible, for a titled Italian family to employ a Gothic letter as its mark. The present duchess of Aosta recently wrote that she knew of no collection in her family that employed such a mark, and that the Aosta family has never owned a palace in Brianza. I therefore believe it impossible that the Gothic *A* refers to the Aosta family. For that reason, I do not list the Lugt number each time the mark appears, since it seemed cumbersome to correct the Lugt citation each time. It is likely that the Gothic *A* reflects an Austrian or German provenance for the drawings.

We are pleased to be able to present in this exhibition, the first the Metropolitan has ever devoted entirely to architectural and ornament drawings, a part of our collection that deserves to be much better known.

M. L. M.
October 1974

ACKNOWLEDGEMENTS

I am grateful to Drue E. Heinz, who set up the fund that has substantially supported this exhibition and that has greatly assisted me in carrying out research for this catalogue. Many curators, scholars, and collectors have provided me with information and access to their collections. I deeply appreciate the assistance of Roseline Bacou, Allan Braham, Alessandro Bettagno, Raffaele Causa, Marianne Fischer, Anna Forlani Tempesti, Jörg Garms, Eleanor Garvey, John Gere, Mr. and Mrs. Paul Gourary, Andreina Griseri, Hellmut Hager, John Harris, Sabine Jacob, Diane M. Kelder, Phyllis Lambert, Wolfgang Lotz, Ulrich Middeldorf, Henry A. Millon, Herbert Mitchell, Geneviève Monnier, Maria Teresa Muraro, Mary Newcome, Werner Oechslin, Donald Oenslager, Adolf Placzek, Philip Pouncey, Annegrit Schmidt, Janos Scholz, Nesta Spink, Mercedes Viale Ferrero, Peter Ward-Jackson, Mark Weil, Peter Wick, the late Rudolf Wittkower, and Silla Zamboni. Elaine Evans Dee, Curator of Prints and Drawings at the Cooper-Hewitt Museum, a dear friend and colleague, has been endlessly generous with advice and information. The identification of many drawings in this catalogue resulted from our discussions.

John McKendry not only conceived this exhibition with infectious enthusiasm, his superlative purchases of the past several years made it worth doing. Without his encouragement, aid in arranging research trips, and assistance in a multitude of problems, the exhibition would never have come to pass. The counsel of A. Hyatt Mayor and Janet S. Byrne was constant. In addition, Janet Byrne read the manuscript, and her keen understanding of ornament drawings sharpened many of the entries. My heartfelt thanks go to members of the Department of Prints and Photographs: Colta F. Ives, Weston J. Naef, Suzanne Boorsch, David Kiehl, Edmond Stack, Andrea G. Rawle, Mary Ann Elliott, and Lisa Kernan. Phyllis D. Massar graciously lent her photographs of Juvarra's Antamoro Chapel and helped, as did Olga Sichel, with bibliographical tasks.

I am particularly grateful to Jacob Bean who, over the years, has taught me much and has made the extensive resources of the Department of Drawings available to me. The two drawings lent from that department's collection — the Canaletto (No. 20) and the Vanvitelli (No. 63) — are important additions to the exhibition. Other colleagues in the Museum who have been of assistance to me are Olga Raggio, Anthony M. Clark, James David Draper, Jessie McNab Dennis, Morrison Heckscher, Anna McCann, and Clare Vincent. Marcie Kesner of the Museum's editorial staff worked long and hard with good cheer on the manuscript. Margaret Dunwoody typed the manuscript and aided me in many ways.

Architectural and
Ornament Drawings

Publications Cited in Abbreviated Form

Bean and Stampfle, 1971

Jacob Bean and Felice Stampfle, *Drawings from New York Collections, III: The Eighteenth Century in Italy* (exhibition catalogue), New York, The Metropolitan Museum of Art, The Pierpont Morgan Library, 1971.

Cini, 1970

Maria Teresa Muraro and Elena Povoledo, *Disegni teatrali dei Bibiena* (exhibition catalogue), Venice, Cini Foundation, 1970.

Detroit-Florence, 1974

The Twilight of the Medici: Late Baroque Art in Florence, 1670–1743 (exhibition catalogue), Detroit, The Detroit Institute of Arts, Florence, Palazzo Pitti, 1974.

Garms, 1971

Jörg Garms, "Die Briefe des Luigi Vanvitelli an seinen Bruder Urbano in Rom: Kunsthistorisches Material," *Römische Historische Mitteilungen* XIII, Rome-Vienna, 1971.

Heawood

Edward Heawood, *Watermarks, Mainly of the 17th and 18th Centuries,* Hilversum, 1950.

Lankheit, 1959

K. Lankheit, "Il Giornale del Foggini," *Rivista d'Arte* XXXIV, Florence, 1959, pp. 55–92.

Lugt, Lugt S.

Frits Lugt, *Les Marques de collections de dessins et d'estampes . . .* , Amsterdam, 1921. *Supplément,* The Hague, 1956.

Messina, 1966

Vittorio Viale, *Mostra di Filippo Juvarra, Architetto e Scenografo* (exhibition catalogue), Messina, Università degli Studi di Messina, 1966.

Naples, 1973

Jörg Garms, *Disegni di Luigi Vanvitelli nelle collezioni pubbliche di Napoli e di Caserta* (exhibition catalogue), Naples, Palazzo Reale, 1973.

Philadelphia, 1968

Diane M. Kelder, *Drawings by the Bibiena Family* (exhibition catalogue), Philadelphia, The Philadelphia Museum of Art, 1968.

Portsmouth, 1969

S. Kaufman and George Knox, *Fantastic and Ornamental Drawings: A Selection of Drawings from the Kaufman Collection* (exhibition catalogue), Portsmouth, England, Portsmouth College of Art and Design, 1969.

Rovere, Viale, Brinckmann

L. Rovere, V. Viale, A. E. Brinckmann, *Comitato a Filippo Juvarra . . . Filippo Juvarra,* I, Milan, 1937.

Vanvitelli

Renato de Fusco, Roberto Pane, Arnaldo Venditti, Roberto di Stefano, Franco Strazzullo, and Cesare de' Seta, *Luigi Vanvitelli,* Naples, 1973.

GIOCONDO ALBERTOLLI (attributed to)
(Bedano 1742–1839 Milan)

1 Design for a ceiling decoration

Pen, gray brown ink, with wash. 11½ x 17 in.
(292 x 432 mm)
The Elisha Whittelsey Collection, The Elisha Whittelsey
Fund, 57.582.1

One of the most important taste-makers of his day, Albertolli was the professor of drawing and ornament in the Accademia di Belle Arti di Brera in Milan, where he taught his own brand of neoclassicism to an entire generation from the founding of the academy in 1776 until 1812. He further spread his ideas by publication of his designs in *Ornamenti Diversi . . .* (1782), *Alcune Decorazione di Nobile Sale . . .* (1787), and *Miscellanea per i Giovani studiosi del Disegno . . .* (1796).

The son of an architect, he was sent at the age of eleven from his small town in the Ticino to Parma to study in the academy there. The training provided by the Parma Academy, directed by the Frenchman E. A. Petitot, has been called the best in Italy at that time. After gaining a thorough grounding in architecture and ornamental decoration, Albertolli went to Florence in 1770 and helped in the decorations of the ducal villa, Poggio Imperiale. In 1772 he visited Rome and Naples, where he is said to have met the elderly architect Luigi Vanvitelli and assisted his son, Carlo, with the completion of the church of SS. Annunziata. In 1774 he returned to Northern Italy where he met the great Milanese architect Piermarini, whose assistant he soon became. In his post at the Accademia di Brera (Piermarini was the director), Albertolli taught his version of neoclassic design, based on a strong adherence to a sober, archaeologically correct ornament learned in Rome: it is cool, clear, always restrained, never exuberant or romantic like that of his near contemporary, Felice Giani. His great works are the *stucchi* for the rooms in the Villa Ducale at Monza (1775–79), the Palazzo Melzi in Milan (1805), and the architecture as well as the interior design for Villa Melzi in Bellagio (1808–15).

The attribution of this drawing is a traditional one. The drawing employs the decorative language seen in various plates in Albertolli's engraved works, especially pls. II and XVI in *Ornamenti Diversi*. A drawing by the same artist is in the University of Michigan Museum of Art (R. Wunder, *Architectural and Ornament Drawings of the 16th to the early 19th Centuries in the Collection of The University of Michigan Museum of Art*, Ann Arbor, 1965, no. 65 repr.). Listed simply as North Italian School, the Michigan drawing has Albertolli's name inscribed on the verso. It came from the same Parisian dealer as ours. Six more ceiling designs by the same hand are at the Cooper-Hewitt Museum, according to Richard Wunder.

The only certain drawings connected with Albertolli are preparatory ones for the engravings of furniture and metalwork in his published works (A. Gonzalez-Palacios, "Drawings by Giocondo Albertolli," *Arte Illustrata* IV, 1971, pp. 24–33, with bibliography). As befits drawings for engravings, they are very precisely delineated, quite different in treatment from this ceiling design.

It is always dangerous to attribute drawings on the basis of inscriptions, since they are often unreliable. Moreover, drawings by the same artist in different media and for different purposes can differ so radically as to make it impossible to connect them without outside evidence. However, the ornament in our drawing is very close to that which Albertolli employed, and since the drawing is clearly a working drawing, not a pastiche of someone else's motifs, the attribution is retained.

GIUSEPPE BARBERI
(Rome 1746–1809 Rome)

2 Design for a stage set

Pen, brown ink, with colored wash. 16⅛ x 21¾ in.
(410 x 552 mm)
Inscribed, verso, in red chalk at upper left, *Decors de theatre/ Seppia*(?); in pencil at upper right, *Valadier*

BIBLIOGRAPHY: R. Berliner, "Zeichnungen des römischen Architekten Giuseppe Barberi," *Münchner Jahrbuch der bildenden Kunst* XVI, 1965, pp. 197, 205, fig. 54
The Elisha Whittelsey Collection, The Elisha Whittelsey
Fund, 61.501

A prodigious draughtsman, Barberi designed many architectural projects that remained for the most part unexecuted. He was trained as a silversmith under Luigi Valadier, father of the Roman neoclassic architect, Giuseppe Valadier. Many of Barberi's drawings, including this one, were wrongly attributed to the younger Valadier until Berliner showed them to be the innovative products of Barberi's fertile imagination. Most of Barberi's drawings are in the Cooper-Hewitt Museum and the Museo di Roma. They show Barberi to have been one of Rome's important neoclassic designers. Berliner dates our drawing 1770–80.

This lavishly colored stage set exemplifies Barberi's neoclassic style. The view is straight on: the baroque effect of unending space achieved through the Bibiena's *scena per angolo* is replaced by a clear, carefully defined, enclosed space. Gigantic columns form a frontal screen, behind which a railing reinforces the two-dimensional screen effect. The simplified architectural elements are grandiosely presented on a huge scale. The monumental background is created by a rusticated arcade acting as wings for a simple temple front that consists of a colonnade surmounted by a stepped dome. A chair on a high, stepped platform, suggesting a throne, is at left. Behind it and on the opposite side of the stage are two lions *couchant*.

MAURO BERTI (attributed to)
(Bologna 1772–1842 Bologna)

3 Design for a stage set

Pen, brown ink, with brown and gray wash. 10½ x 8⅛ in. (267 x 206 mm). Laid down with narrow French mount pasted on top of drawing with a Gothic A stamped in purple ink at lower right of mount

PROVENANCE: S. Kaufman, London
EXHIBITIONS: Portsmouth, 1969, no. 55, repr.
Harris Brisbane Dick Fund and Joseph Pulitzer Bequest, 1971.513.67

This drawing has the same characteristics as one in the Kunstbibliothek in Berlin (H. Schmitz, *Baumeisterzeichnungen des 17. und 18. Jahrhunderts ...*, Berlin and Leipzig [1937], pl. 20) traditionally attributed to Mauro Berti, the Bolognese stage designer. The drawings are certainly by the same hand, the only question being if that hand is indeed Mauro Berti's. Both drawings have dramatic, soaring flights of stairs and heavy, rusticated architecture, although the Berlin drawing employs Gothic arches, while ours uses columns that support a classically coffered ceiling with the suggestion of a Pantheon-like domed space. The two different architectural styles, however, are both rendered in the same romantic fashion, and both have the dramatic contrasts of light and shade for which Berti was noted. The Berlin drawing is quite close to an engraving of Berti's set of the interior of a castle (L. Ruggi, *Raccolta inedita di cinquanta scene teatrali ...*, Bologna [about 1825], pl. VI).

4 Design for a stage set

Pen, brown ink, with brown and gray wash. 10¾ x 8 in. (273 x 203 mm). Laid down with narrow French mount pasted on top of drawing
Gift of Cornelius Vanderbilt, 80.3.621

Here attributed to Berti for the first time, this design shares the same distinctive architectural motifs with No. 3, especially the freestanding, soaring stairways and the tendency toward romanticized classical and Gothic forms, as well as the same style of pen- and brushwork.

CARLO BIANCONI
(Bologna 1732–1802 Milan)

5 Design for a cartouche with two putti, an eagle, a lion's head, and a grotesque mask

Pen and brown ink. 7 x 8⅝ in. (178 x 219 mm). Laid down on old French mount with a Gothic A stamped in purple ink at lower right

PROVENANCE: Janos Scholz, New York
The Elisha Whittelsey Collection, The Elisha Whittelsey Fund, 52.570.103

Bianconi was a member of a learned Bolognese family whose father, a doctor and archaeologist, was a host to Winckelmann on his first visit to Italy. Carlo became not only a notable decorative painter and engraver but continued his father's interest in archaeology, seriously studying antique monuments while on a trip to Rome in 1777–78: an interest documented by a drawing in the Uffizi of an antique frieze, signed with his monogram and dated 1777 (inv. no. 43195). Carlo Bianconi was, moreover, the author of the much amplified edition of Malvasia's artistic guide to Bologna as well as a guidebook to Milan, where he lived from 1778. He was at the center of artistic life there as perpetual secretary of the Accademia di Belle Arti di Brera. While in Bologna, he worked closely with Mauro Tesi (Nos. 57, 58), in 1764 designing with Tesi the monument in the Campo Santo, Pisa, to their mutual benefactor, Count Algarotti, and in 1767 a monument in S. Petronio to Tesi, after Tesi's death the previous year. (For a bibliography of Bianconi by S. Samek Ludovici, see *Dizionario Enciclopedico Bolaffi dei Pittori e degli incisori italiani ...*, II, Turin, 1972, pp. 246–248.)

Identified by Richard Wunder, this drawing conforms to the many cartouche designs by Bianconi in the Cooper-Hewitt Museum. A design for a frieze there (acc. no. 1938-88-3277) is laid down on a mount with the same format as our drawing.

6 Sketch for a cartouche with grotesque masks and harpy

Pen and brown ink. 7¹¹⁄₁₆ x 8½ in. (179 x 216 mm). A border of gray green ink on the sheet itself with a Gothic A stamped in purple ink at lower left

PROVENANCE: Janos Scholz, New York
The Elisha Whittelsey Collection, The Elisha Whittelsey Fund, 52.570.312

This design, similar in format to No. 5 and probably a study for the same series, has the bite and drama of the best of Bianconi's rapid penwork.

7 Sketch with two masks: a satyr's head and winged Medusa's head

Pen and brown ink. 5¾ x 4¼ in. (146 x 108 mm). Laid down on paper with gold border with a Gothic A stamped in purple ink on mount at lower right. Unidentified collector's mark stamped in black ink on drawing at lower right

PROVENANCE: Janos Scholz, New York
The Elisha Whittelsey Collection, The Elisha Whittelsey Fund, 52.570.313

Probably a study for components of a cartouche like No. 6, and employing the same spirited and powerful penwork, this drawing was, before its attribution to Bianconi, classified as possibly by Ubaldo Gandolfi. In fact, Bianconi's drawing style does derive from Ubaldo's, as a comparison with the drawing in the collection of Mr. and Mrs. A. Hyatt Mayor, New York, reveals (Bean and Stampfle, 1971, no. 286, repr.).

8 Design for a cartouche surmounted by a lion's head in scrollwork suspending swags of fruit and leaves

Black chalk. 8⅞ x 6⅜ in. (225 x 162 mm). Vertical crease at center marked by black chalk line with slits at top and bottom
Inscribed in black chalk at lower left, *Carlo Bianc. inven*
Rogers Fund, 68.774.1

A working drawing in black chalk supplied to Pio Panfili, who engraved it, this is a much more carefully studied drawing than Nos. 5, 6, or 7. Along with the drawings by Sebastiano Cavina (Nos. 21a and b), it was published in Panfili's *Raccolta di Cartelle pubblicate per uso della gioventù studiosa* (Bologna, 1795–98) as pl. 7, dated 1796.

ANTONIO GALLI BIBIENA
(Parma 1697–1774[?] Milan)

9 Study for an interior

Pen, brown ink, over traces of black chalk. 10 x 8 in. (254 x 203 mm). Lightly stained. Inlaid into modern paper

Verso: Sketches for decoration. Brown ink over black chalk, with small numbers in red chalk

PROVENANCE: S. Kaufman, London
EXHIBITIONS: Philadelphia, 1968, no. 5, repr.; Portsmouth, 1969, no. 64, repr.
Harris Brisbane Dick Fund and Joseph Pulitzer Bequest, 1971.513.73

Nos. 9–17 are all associated with members of the Bibiena family or with their workshops. Italy produced a number of families of theatrical designers, among whom were the Galliari of Turin (No. 31) and the Quaglio of north Italy who worked in Austria and southern Germany. The earliest were the Bibienas, who created a new iconography for the stage. Through their travels they spread their style across Europe. The family consisted of: the two brothers, Ferdinando (1657–1743) and Francesco (1659–1739); Ferdinando's sons, Alessandro (1686–1748), Giuseppe (1695–1757), Antonio (1697–1774?), and Giovanni Maria the younger (1700–1777?); Francesco's son, Giovanni Carlo (1713?–1760); and Giuseppe's son, Carlo (1721–1787). This family of prolific artists worked so closely with one

another that it is often difficult for modern eyes to distinguish each artist's work. On many sheets, a drawing by one Bibiena is inscribed by another, thus confusing the identification of both their handwriting and draughtsmanship (for a comparison of their handwriting and draughtsmanship, see H. Leclerc, "Les Bibiena: une dynastie de scénographes baroques," *Revue d'Histoire du Théâtre* XXV, no. 1, 1971, pp. 7–39). As an example of the family's close collaboration, Giuseppe was chief assistant to his father when Ferdinando was theater architect at the Imperial Court in Vienna.

The number of drawings associated with the Bibienas is enormous. They range in style from jotted ideas for ambiguous projects to highly finished designs for stage sets and architecture. There are groups of drawings that are securely identified, while others are cavalierly ascribed to the Bibienas merely because they are baroque eighteenth-century stage sets. Recent work has helped clarify what is one of the most difficult problems in drawings connoisseurship. The books by A. Hyatt Mayor (*The Bibiena Family*, New York, 1945), Diane M. Kelder (Philadelphia, 1968), and Maria Teresa Muraro and Elena Povoledo (Cini, 1970), have presented a great number of drawings with astute discussions that have illumined many unclear issues. What yet remains to be done is to sort out the many drawings in the numerous albums containing sketches made by the Bibienas. The most studied album is that in the Theater Collection of the Österreichischen Nationalbibliothek, Vienna, published by Frans Hadamowsky (*Die Familie Galli-Bibiena in Wien*, Vienna, 1962). There are two volumes in the Bibliotheca Sarti, Accademia di S. Luca, Rome (Cini, 1970, no. 62, one sheet repr.), one in the Houghton Library, Harvard University, one in the Donald Oenslager collection, New York, and one formerly with Wildenstein Gallery, New York (Philadelphia, 1968, nos. 28, 56, 17).

Nos. 9 and 10 are briefly sketched first ideas, typical of the drawings in the Bibiena albums and especially of those in the Vienna, Rome, and Houghton albums. Kaufman and Knox associated No. 9 with Ferdinando and No. 10 with Francesco (Portsmouth, 1969, nos. 64, 41). No. 9 was attributed on the basis of comparison with drawings in the Accademia di S. Luca albums that Kaufman and Knox apparently thought to be entirely by Ferdinando. However, Muraro and Povoledo have shown that a number of the drawings in these albums were made by Giuseppe while in Vienna (Cini, 1970, no. 62). What appears certainly to be work by the same hand as No. 9 is on the recto of leaf 20 in the Houghton album. It depicts an arch and its decoration, is inscribed *Portale* (?)*d[i] Michaeli/ Anno 1739,* and is drawn with the same feel for the curving line as No. 9. The decoration shows a similar reliance on scrolls and urns. On the verso is a sketch of an arched space which includes brief delineations of figures very close to those in No. 10. It is drawn in a style distinctly different from that on the recto. Instead of the recto's curvilinear style, the verso shows a brusque and rectilinear one very similar to that in No. 10.

The drawings in the Houghton album are also associated with Viennese projects of the Bibienas (Cini, 1970, no. 90). By 1739, only Giuseppe and Antonio remained in the Austrian capital, Ferdinando and Francesco having long since left for Italy. Because of the similarity of No. 9 to the drawing in the Houghton album dated 1739, I believe it should be associated with a member of the second-generation Bibienas—Giuseppe or Antonio—rather than Ferdinando or Francesco. In addition, because of the appearance on one sheet of paper of the two distinct styles exhibited in Nos. 9 and 10, I believe that they are by the same artist—most likely, Antonio. Kaufman and Knox noted the resemblance of No. 9 to a drawing in the Philadelphia Museum of Art of a large hall that Kelder attributed to Antonio (Philadelphia, 1968, no. 64, repr.). The architecture and curvilinear character of the drawing are very close to No. 9. Hadamowsky defined Antonio's drawing style as more nervous and detailed than Giuseppe's; it is certainly more mannered.

The volume of drawings in the Oenslager collection has convincingly been shown to be by Antonio (Cini, 1970, no. 108; and Leclerc, "Les Bibiena," pp. 30–32, pl. XXII). The character of its brusque, angular sketches is completely in keeping with No. 10.

In addition, since leaf 20 verso of the Houghton album incorporates in its essentially rectilinear sketchiness some of Antonio's preference for curves in the details of the volutes, and also contains decorative elements like urns which are so characteristic of No. 9, I believe it shows a combination of the two strikingly different modes of draughtsmanship represented by Nos. 9 and 10. This further demonstrates that they are by the same person, namely, Antonio.

Other drawings that are close to No. 9 are, as Kelder pointed out, several sheets in the Vienna Album (Hadamowsky, "Die Familie Galli-Bibiena," pl. 25, leaf 37 verso, and pl. 82, leaf 136 verso). The composition is not far from a leaf in the Accademia di S. Luca album that depicts a vaulted room decorated with huge vases (Vol. II, leaf 24, no. 176). Extremely close in draughtsmanship is a drawing of the interior of a court in the Kunstbibliothek, Berlin (Hdz 1406).

10 Sketch for a stage set

Pen and brown ink. 7¼ x 5 1/16 in. (184 x 129 mm). Laid down and inlaid into modern paper

PROVENANCE: S. Kaufman, London

EXHIBITIONS: Philadelphia, 1968, no. 19, repr.; Portsmouth, 1969, no. 41, repr.
Harris Brisbane Dick Fund and Joseph Pulitzer Bequest, 1971.513.57

For a discussion of the attribution of this drawing, see No. 9.

While I believe that this drawing is by Antonio Bibiena, it must be noted that it is extremely close to several sheets attributed to Francesco. The most striking similarity, both in architecture and draughtsmanship, is with a drawing in the Berlin Kupferstichkabinet (inv. no. 18024) of an arcaded palace courtyard. The viewpoint, the attenuated, sketchy figures, and the distinctive columns with their heavy rustication are the same in both drawings. Two further drawings attributed to Francesco, both in the Cini Foundation, Venice, are in the same rectilinear style (inv. nos. 31.513, 31.519).

There are schematic drawings in the Accademia di S. Luca album that have the same viewpoint and shorthand designation for figures (Vol. II, leaf 7, nos. 138, 139 recto and verso). Also close to our drawing is one in the Uffizi (inv. no. 110628), which, while having rusticated columns, depicts an interior whose details are treated in a freer manner than ours, as on leaf 20 verso in the Houghton album. Leaf 116 recto in the Houghton album, showing a courtyard leading into a long gallery, also resembles No. 10 in the rusticated columns, stairs, and abbreviated figures.

FRANCESCO GALLI BIBIENA (workshop)
(Bologna 1659–1739 Bologna)

11 Proscenium, ceiling, and ground plan of the Nancy theater

Pen, brown ink, with brown wash. 16 7/16 x 20⅝ in. (418 x 524 mm). Vertical crease at center. Inlaid into Arches paper. Watermark: near Heawood 2971
Inscribed in brown ink at top, *Spaccato del Anfiteatro in facia al Prosienio, come ancora lá Inscrizione della Cartella A Sui Suorum; et./ Sui Suorum ciuium/ Voluptati comodo,/ Leopoldi Primi Largitate,/ Francisi Bibiena Italo,/ Bononiensis, Arte/ Teatrum/ Año 1709.;* and below in plan, reading left to right; *Dal Terrapieno delle Mura della Citá posono/ venire nel Teatro Carozze, é Carri per lá/ Porta C/; A Porte che dá ogni ordine di Loggie vano alla Schala á Lumaca./ B Porte della Schala Lumaca che vá dal baso al alto./; Logo per tenervi le Scene che non/ occupino il Palco/; Pianta rustica de Muri/ Sopra de quali posano li legni in piedi che soste/ ngono le loggie del/ Anfiteatro; A Porte del Anfiteatro;* parts of the drawing are inscribed, *Prosienio; Suffitto;* and *Pianta del Teatro di Nancij;* scale above plan, *Schala di Piedi cento di Parigi. Sono di Bologna Piedi 86*

Bequest of Joseph H. Durkee, by exchange, 1972.713.60

The Metropolitan Museum recently acquired Nos. 11–17 in a group of seventy-two previously unknown drawings, all except one associated with the work of members of the Bibiena family. The drawings are said to have come from an unidentified Parisian collection. Most are for catafalques: plans, elevations, and sections. There are also stage sets and designs for the decoration of theater interiors and exteriors as well as decorations for church festivities, or *Theatra Sacra*. Most appear to be preparations for engravings made by shop assistants. Several members of the family had their drawings engraved; in many cases it is the only record of their work. Ferdinando produced examples of his innovative stage sets—*scene per angolo*—in his treatises *Varie opere di Prospettiva* (Bologna, 1703–08) and *L'Architettura Civile* (Parma, 1711); Francesco had engravings made of his theater in the Hofburg, Vienna, and projected them for his Teatro Filarmonico in Verona (now destroyed), while Giuseppe produced a record of stage sets, catafalques, and *Theatra Sacra* in his *Architetture, e prospettive* (Augsburg, 1740), to which a number of our drawings are related.

No. 11 is a preparatory drawing. Unlike engravings of projects such as catafalques, made as records of temporary structures, the engraving to be made from this drawing was to have commemorated a permanent building: the theater at Nancy built for Leopold, duke of Lorraine, between April 1708 and November 1709 (on the Nancy theater, see F. G. Pariset, "L'Opéra de Nancy de François Bibiena (1708–1709)," *Urbanisme et architecture: Mélanges P. Lavedan,* Paris, 1954, pp. 277–285; and M. Antoine, "L'Opéra de Nancy," *Le Pays Lorrain* XLVI, no. 1, 1965, pp. 1–23). Other drawings for this theater are in the Musée Historique Lorrain, Nancy, the Museu Nacional de Arte Antiga, Lisbon, and the Louvre (see Cini, 1970, nos. 44–47). The drawings in Nancy are Francesco's first project, and those at Lisbon, his second and final one. The Louvre drawings are shop copies of the Lisbon series.

Francesco was the first member of the family to build theaters as well as to design sets. In 1699–1700 (Hadamowsky, *Die Familie Galli-Bibiena,* p. 9) he completely renovated the theater in the Hofburg, Vienna, for Emperor Leopold I (theater destroyed in 1747). The Hoftheater's architecture greatly influenced theater design in Germany and Austria throughout the first half of the eighteenth century. Muraro and Povoledo (Cini, 1970, no. 48) stressed its influence on Francesco's nephew, Giuseppe Bibiena, when he designed his theater at Bayreuth.

Although the court of Lorraine depended on French architects, Duke Leopold's choice of Francesco to design the theater must have been due to the success of his Hoftheater and the predominance of Italian over French architects in the field of stage design at that period.

Francesco arrived in Lorraine at the end of 1707. By the following spring his plans were ready, but work that had begun on the foundations was held up because he had radically altered his designs. That alteration is documented in the difference between the Nancy and Lisbon drawings. The Nancy drawings show that the original auditorium (*anfiteatro* on our plan) was round. Francesco retained the same width but lengthened the auditorium into an ellipse and also probably raised its height. The drawing of the ceiling at Lisbon (inv. no. 220; Cini, 1970, no. 47, repr.) shows the auditorium's basic elliptical shape as well as its ceiling decoration. A full drawing of the proscenium (inv. no. 314; ibid., no. 44, repr.), a longitudinal section (inv. no. 219; ibid., no. 45), and a transverse section showing the entrance and ducal box (inv. no. 219a) all agree with our drawings, although certain details differ slightly, for instance, the decorations of the railings of the boxes. What had not been known from the Lisbon sheets but has come to light with our drawings, was the detailed plan of the entire structure. A ground plan of 1748 in the Nancy Archives showing the plan of the structural walls without details (Antoine, "L'Opéra de Nancy," p. 16, repr.) seems to support an observation of Henry A. Millon, who pointed out to me the resemblance of the plan of the theater to a church. The projecting areas adjacent to the proscenium and stage look like church transepts appended to a long nave and chancel. The walls of one of these projections, labeled on our drawing *logo per tenervi le scene* (storage area for the flats), abuts a Franciscan convent. The theater therefore was probably built on the foundations of the convent's church, but since neither Pariset nor Antoine gives documentary evidence for the existence of a church on the site, this hypothesis lacks proof.

No. 11 depicts, reading top left to right, half a transverse section of the main entrance and ducal box, half the proscenium and the decoration of the curtain, half the ceiling of the auditorium with its decoration, and at the bottom, a full ground plan. Our drawing of the entrance gives the inscription in the cartouche that surmounts it; this is illegible in the Lisbon sheet except for the date, 1708, which differs from ours. The difference suggests that our drawings were made on completion of the building in November 1709. With that in mind, the variation between the Lisbon sheet and ours in the details of the treatment of the strapwork railings of the boxes suggests that ours represents the final version as erected. In addition, the decoration of the walls of the boxes, blank in the Lisbon drawing, is fully delineated in ours. The stage and its curtain vary slightly in the two versions. The columns flanking the proscenium in our drawing lack the fluting seen in the Lisbon sheet. There are, as well, slight variations in the treatment of the scroll brackets supporting the proscenium arch. Prominent in both drawings are Leopold's arms and crown and the cross of Lorraine. The large trophy in the center of the curtain is difficult to distinguish in our drawing, as only half of it appears. It employs references to the arts of painting, music, and drama, as well as the military arts. The ceiling in the Lisbon drawing agrees with ours, but is complete, and shows more clearly its decoration and disposition into panels connected with rich, intertwining foliage. The ground plan in our drawing shows that the deep stage has an entrance at the back, labeled as being for carriages. In the Nancy Archives ground plan, that entrance is also designated as for the artists.

It was Francesco's practice to plan engravings of his theaters. The Hoftheater was engraved in 1704 by Pfeffel and Engelbrecht. Joseph Chamant prepared drawings (now in the Cooper-Hewitt Museum, acc. nos. 1938–54–1413, 1443; Mayor, *The Bibiena Family*, pls. 20, 21) of Francesco's Teatro Filarmonico that were not engraved. Muraro observed that our drawings, clearly preparations for engravings, are very close to Francesco's draughtsmanship as it is known from the Lisbon drawings. The Lisbon sheets are inscribed in what is taken to be his handwriting. There are variations in the handwriting between our drawings and those in Lisbon, but that in ours is extremely close to the precise hand of the Lisbon sheets. It may be significant, however, that on the Lisbon sheets Nancy is spelled *Nansi* and on ours, *Nancij*, indicating they were drawn by two different artists. The figures in No. 11 (and in No. 12, too) lack the rotundity of those in the Lisbon drawings: it must be kept in mind that the Bibienas often drew the architecture and left the figures to an assistant. There is also a greater precision and authority in the calligraphic flourishes of the Lisbon drawings. If our drawings are not by Francesco himself, he must have overseen their execution very closely, imposing his style. This was, after all, the family's shop practice.

The history of the Nancy theater is unfortunate. Because Louis XIV's troops had occupied Nancy in 1709, Duke Leopold had removed the court to Lunéville, and was not on hand for the theater's inauguration. Hostilities persisted until 1714 when Leopold and the court returned to Nancy. Although there were several performances in the theater, the duke had far outspent his means, and there was little money for more of his lavish entertainments. After 1737, when Lorraine was ceded to France and the dukes of Lorraine were given Tuscany in recompense, Francis Stephen of Lorraine stripped the decorations of the theater to take with him to Tuscany. Joseph Chamant, who had gone to Italy in 1724 to work in Francesco's studio, was in charge of their installation in a theater in Florence, probably the Teatro della Pergola. The rest of the loges were soon removed to Lunéville. During the War of the Austrian Succession part of the theater was turned into a military storehouse, and later the whole was used as a barracks. It was completely destroyed in 1818. Our drawings are therefore the most complete record of the theater now known, as engravings for the Nancy theater have not come to light, and seemingly were never made.

12 Longitudinal section and half ground plan for the Nancy theater

Pen, brown ink, with brown wash. 16¼ x 20³⁄₁₆ in. (413 x 513 mm). Inlaid into Arches paper. Watermark: near Heawood 2971
Inscribed in brown ink at bottom, within plan, reading right to left, *Pianta del Teatro di Nancij; G Apertura sul Palco per i Lumi./ F Orchestra per li Sonatori./ D Loggie private per Sua A ª Reale, o/ per le Dame di Sua A ª Reale./ H Schale che vano sul Palco del/ Teatro./; A Gran Loggia per Sua Altezza Reale./ Q Porta, et sito per le aque Rinfrescative et altre./ B Schale che vano dal baso al alto. E Loggie con Gelosie per/ Religiosi. C Loggie che Servono nel Piano nobile per li/ Cavaglieri di S.A.R.ˡᵉ. A Porte del Anfiteatro.;* scale within middle of plan, *Schala di Piedi venticinque di Parigi,* and below *Schala di Piedi venticinque di Bologna.*
Bequest of Joseph H. Durkee, by exchange, 1972.713.61

For a discussion of the Nancy theater, see No. 11.

The area designated *Q* on the plan is for refreshments. *A* is the ducal box; *E*, next to it, is reserved for the clergy. *D* is a private loge either for the duke or ladies of the court. *F* is for the orchestra. The ground plan is placed below the corresponding parts in the section where they are shown in elevation; thus, the plan of the private loge *D* is directly below the large loge, two levels high with an imposing canopy. The slope of the stage and the placement of the flats are clearly seen at right.

GIUSEPPE GALLI BIBIENA (workshop)
(Parma 1695–1757 Berlin)

13 Design for a *Theatrum Sacrum*

Pen, brown ink, with gray and rose wash, over black chalk. 22¹³⁄₁₆ x 16¾ in. (579 x 426 mm). Horizontal crease at center. Inlaid into Arches paper. Watermark: near Heawood 3021
Bequest of Joseph H. Durkee, by exchange, 1972.713.51

One of Giuseppe Bibiena's responsibilities as Principal Theater Architect for the Austrian court was to design decorations for church celebrations. He included several of these *Theatra Sacra* in his *Architetture, e prospettive*. Most of the drawings from the group of which No. 13 is a part are related to projects that Giuseppe had engraved in *Architetture, e prospettive*. It seems clear from the evidence of our drawings that subsequent volumes were planned: the book was divided into five parts, and on the verso of one of our drawings is an inscription describing it as for the seventh (acc. no. 1972.713.8).

This *Theatrum Sacrum* was not engraved, but is closest to that represented in *Architetture, e prospettive*, II, pl. 5. There, the architecture is far more complicated, but the depiction of scenes of the Passion is similar to No. 13. In our drawing, Pilate, washing his hands, appears on the top step, below whom the Flagellation of Christ is depicted as

He is led down the stairs by a soldier. Another scene from the Passion, represented simultaneously as in a medieval mystery play, is the Carrying of the Cross, which is seen at far right. Statues of Hercules stand atop the balustrades flanking Pilate. The statue above the doorway at left, holding a torch, alludes to the goddesses Demeter and Persephone, symbolizing death and rebirth. Atop the doorway at right is a statue of Diana, goddess of the moon and of the hunt.

The Bibiena shop practice of using one artist specializing in architecture, and another in figures, is employed here.

14 Design for a stage set

Pen, brown ink, with gray wash, over black chalk.
17½ x 22¼ in. (445 x 565 mm). Stained, some tears, repaired. Arches paper cut away leaving only ¼ in. strip pasted to edges of verso. Vertical crease at center
Bequest of Joseph H. Durkee, by exchange, 1972.713.64

The lack of detail on this unfinished drawing gives it a neoclassic appearance, and thus suggests a later date than may be warranted, as a drawing exhibiting neoclassic elements is more likely to be associated with a member of the third generation of the Bibiena family than an earlier one.

Two designs, one in the Zurcher collection, Chicago, and the other in the Cleveland Museum of Art, exhibit a similar spatial sense, although they are more highly finished and depict more ornate interiors. They were both attributed to Giuseppe Bibiena by Kelder (Philadelphia, 1968, nos. 42, 43, repr.). A sheet in the Vienna album, leaves 137 verso and 138 recto, shows a palace corridor quite similar to the one in No. 14: this sheet also depicts a coffered barrel vault, but instead of classical busts, full-length statues line the walls (Hadamowsky, *Die Familie Galli-Bibiena*, pl. 92).

Although No. 14 does have certain affinities with the work of Carlo Bibiena (see Philadelphia, 1968, nos. 67, 68, 71–73, repr.), I believe that its similarity to the Vienna sheet connects the author of the composition to one of the draughtsmen of the Vienna album, thereby excluding Carlo. It is probable that this drawing reflects a project of Carlo's father, Giuseppe.

15 Elevation of the catafalque for Empress Eleonora of Austria

Pen, brown ink, with gray wash, over traces of black chalk. Lightly squared for transfer in black chalk. 31 x 23⅜ in. (787 x 543 mm). Two horizontal creases at center, the lower one mended
Bequest of Joseph H. Durkee, by exchange, 1972.713.32

This catafalque corresponds to the only unidentified catafalque in Giuseppe's *Architetture, e prospettive,* V, pls. 1, 2. The only clue to its identity is the Austrian double-headed eagle in the cartouche on pl. 1. A drawing in the Metropolitan for the ground plan of this catafalque (acc. no. 1972.713.31) has an inscription that identifies it as commemorating Empress Eleonora Magdalena Theresa (1655–1720), wife of Emperor Leopold I (died 1705). Hadamowsky cited documents that list Giuseppe as the designer of Empress Eleonora's catafalque (*Die Familie Galli-Bibiena,* p. 22). Our drawing corresponds in its perspective viewpoint to the second engraving. Both engravings omit the high structures supporting statues that flank the catafalque. Another difference between the drawing and engravings is the change in the pediment surmounting the central arch.

The draughtsmanship of the architecture is very close to that in No. 13 and may be by the same shop assistant.

16 Ground plan of the catafalque for Anna Cristina, wife of Carlo Emanuele III of Savoy

Pen, brown ink, with gray wash. 20¾ x 14¼ in.
(527 x 362 mm). Inlaid into Arches paper. Watermark: near Heawood 1835
Inscribed, recto, in brown ink at upper left, *18*; verso, at top, *Anna Cristina Regina di Sardegna*
Bequest of Joseph H. Durkee, by exchange, 1972.713.19

In 1722, Anna Cristina of Bavaria married Carlo Emanuele III of the house of Savoy, who became, in 1730, king of Sardinia. Anna Cristina died the year after her marriage. There is no record that Giuseppe designed a catafalque for the Hapsburg's commemoration of her death, but this drawing indicates that one was erected in her honor. The fact that Anna Cristina is designated queen of Sardinia, although she never held the title, suggests that this drawing, preparatory for the engraver, was made after 1730. It is also possible that this catafalque was for Carlo Emanuele's second wife, Polissena Cristina of Hesse, who died in 1735. The inscription in that case could be explained as confusion between the two wives' names. The drawing must have been intended for a later volume of *Architetture, e prospettive* and therefore probably dates about 1740. There is no similar catafalque ground plan, either in our drawings or in the engravings in the *Architetture, e prospettive,* that is shown in projection as is this one.

In addition to our fifty-one drawings of catafalques, there are a number of others in various collections, many of which are related to ours. The best known, in the Royal Institute of British Architects, is for the elevation of the catafalque for Francis Lewis of Neuburg, archbishop of

Mainz, died 1732 (engraved in *Architetture, et prospettive,* I, pl. 3; published by R. Blomfield, *Architectural Drawings and Draughtsmen,* London, 1912, third pl. following p. 62) for which we possess the ground plan (acc. no. 1972.713.30). This drawing is inscribed in exactly the same fashion as some of our other catafalques and has always been assumed to be the contemporary preparation for the engraving. Other catafalques are in the Kunstbibliothek, Berlin (Hdz 534, 5011, 4542, 4541), the first three of which are related to three of ours, and the last related to one at Avery Library (AAZ39).

17 Elevation and section of the catafalque for Anna Cristina, wife of Carlo Emanuele III of Savoy

Pen, brown ink, with gray wash. 20¾ x 14¹³⁄₁₆ in.
(527 x 376 mm). Inlaid into Arches paper. Watermark: near Heawood 1835
Inscribed, recto, in brown ink at upper left, *18*; verso, at top, *Anna Cristina Regina di Sardegna*
Bequest of Joseph H. Durkee, by exchange, 1972.713.20

For a discussion of this catafalque, see No. 16.

GIUSEPPE BERNARDINO BISON
(Palmanova, Friuli 1762–1844 Milan)

18 Design for wall decoration

Pen, brown ink, with brown and colored wash. 8 x 6¹⁄₁₆ in.
(203 x 154 mm)
PROVENANCE: According to dealer, Ferruccio Asta, Venice (no mark, see Lugt S 116a) and Cernazai
The Elisha Whittelsey Collection, The Elisha Whittelsey Fund, 67.707.1

Bison was the last painter in the great tradition of Venetian eighteenth-century decoration. He studied at Brescia and in Venice where he was in the studio of Anton Maria Zanetti. He remained in Venice until 1807, when he left for Trieste. His last years, 1831–44, were spent in Milan. Many of his drawings are in the collection of the Castello Sforzesco, Milan, and he is well represented with a number of sheets in the Cooper-Hewitt Museum. (For further information and bibliography, see A. Rizzi, *Cento disegni del Bison* [exhibition catalogue], Udine, 1962–63).

The panel of arabesque ornament at right, reminiscent of Tiepolo's style, points to a date early in Bison's career when he decorated many villas in the Veneto. Bison's work became increasingly neoclassic over the years, and his late drawings are quick and angular, in gray rather than colored wash.

SERAFINO BRIZZI (attributed to)
(Bologna 1684–1737 Bologna)

19 Design for a stage set

Pen, brown ink, with gray wash. 6¼ x 9⅛ in.
(159 x 232 mm)
PROVENANCE: A. P. E. Gasc, Paris (his mark at lower right, Lugt 1131); S. Kaufman, London
EXHIBITIONS: Portsmouth, 1969, no. 56, repr.
Harris Brisbane Dick Fund and Joseph Pulitzer Bequest, 1971.513.68

Brizzi was not only a stage designer, as shown by this drawing, but also a painter, engraver, and *quadraturista*. In addition, he was a costume designer and actor.

The influence of the Bibienas on Brizzi, a pupil of Ferdinando Bibiena, is evident in this design, an elaborated derivation of a drawing of a prison scene in the Bibiena sketchbook in the Accademia di S. Luca, Rome (Vol. I, leaf 11). The S. Luca drawing lacks the pointed arches and hanging lantern of our drawing. The prison scene in Ferdinando Bibiena's *Varie opere di Prospettiva* (etched by Pietro Giovanni Abbati, pl. 12) is a precursor of the Metropolitan's drawing; however, it depicts only two arches joined at the center, and is viewed from a much closer viewpoint, creating a more dramatic, even claustrophobic scene.

CANALETTO
(GIOVANNI ANTONIO CANAL)
(Venice 1697–1768 Venice)

20 Architectural *capriccio*

Pen, brown ink, with gray wash. 15 x 21¼ in.
(318 x 540 mm)
Inscribed with false signature at lower left, *Canaletto*

PROVENANCE: Baron Dominique Vivant Denon, Paris, his mark at bottom right (Lugt 779); Earl of Warwick, Warwick Castle, Warwick, his mark twice at bottom, left and right (Lugt 2600)
EXHIBITIONS: Toronto, Art Gallery, *Canaletto*, 1964, p. 119, pl. 98 (also shown Ottawa, National Gallery of Canada and Montreal, Museum of Fine Arts with the same catalogue)
BIBLIOGRAPHY: Amaury Duval, *Monuments des Arts du dessin . . . recueillis par le baron Vivant Denon,* II, Paris, 1829, pl. 150; W. G. Constable, *Canaletto,* I, Oxford, 1962, pl. 152, fig. 807; II, p. 554, no. 807; Bean and Stampfle, 1971, no. 160
Harris Brisbane Dick Fund, 46.161

Canaletto is said to have arrived at his career as *vedutista*, or painter of views, at about the time of his trip to Rome in 1719. There he devoted himself to studying and drawing actual views, giving up his earlier métier of designing stage sets, which he had learned from his scenographer father. Returning to Venice, he perfected the painting of *vedute,* in addition to modifying the genre by painting imaginary scenes such as this one. As a form, the *capriccio* bridges the two genres Canaletto worked in. It incorporates fantasy views with scattered architectural motifs, like a stage set, yet also depicts actual architectural monuments, like a *veduta.* The scene in this drawing is distinctly Venetian despite the Roman arch that stands alongside a Gothic tower amidst broken columns and other ruins. This arch, as Constable noted (*Canaletto,* II, p. 554, no. 807), resembles that of Septimius Severus, recalling Canaletto's Roman sojourn.

Vivant Denon, who once owned this drawing, was France's Director General of Fine Arts under Napoleon and curator of his growing collection of Europe's plundered art installed in the Louvre. It is interesting that Vivant Denon, an arbiter of taste during the Empire, with its neoclassic ideals, would value this almost rococo *capriccio* so highly as to include it in the planned publication of his collection *Monuments des Arts du dessin.* Published posthumously, this work contained four lithograph illustrations of Vivant Denon's drawings by Canaletto, this one and another (II, pl. 148; Bean and Stampfle, 1971, no. 155, repr.) also in the Metropolitan's Department of Drawings (acc. no. 43.61).

An architectural *capriccio* close to No. 20 was exhibited at the Metropolitan Museum (Bean and Stampfle, 1971, no. 160, repr.). It employed a combination of Roman and Gothic elements, and its execution was carried out in a similar manner.

A contemporary copy of No. 20 is in the William Rockhill Nelson Gallery of Art, Kansas City.

SEBASTIANO CAVINA
(Bologna, active 1790s)

21a and b Designs for cartouches

(a) Cartouche with a cornucopia of fruit and leaves surmounted by a grotesque mask in scrollwork crowned with garlands
Pen, brown ink over black chalk. 9¹/₁₆ x 6¹³/₁₆ in.
(230 x 173 mm). Vertical crease at center marked faintly with black chalk line with slits at top and bottom
Inscribed in brown ink at lower left, *Sebasᵒ Cavina A:C: Inv*

(b) Cartouche with swags at sides and bottom surmounted by a mask set between two rosettes
Pen, brown ink, over black chalk. 9⁵/₁₆ x 6¾ in.
(237 x 171 mm). Vertical crease at center marked faintly with black chalk line with slits at top and bottom
Inscribed in brown ink at lower left, *Sebasᵒ Cavina A:C: Inv*
Rogers Fund, 68.774.2,3

The little-known Cavina is best remembered for his designs for ornament prints. A draughtsman, engraver, sculptor, and goldsmith, he drew these cartouches for Panfili's *Raccolta di Cartelle pubblicate per uso della gioventù studiosa,* based on the example of his Bolognese predecessor Agostino Mitelli and the Florentine Stefano della Bella. 21a was engraved as pl. 10, dated 1797, and 21b as pl. 11, dated 1796.

GREGORIO DE FERRARI
(Portomaurizio 1647–1726 Genoa)

22 Ceiling design with the Presentation in the Temple

Pen, brown ink, with brown wash, heightened with white on blue gray paper. 20¾ x 16¼ in. (527 x 413 mm)
BIBLIOGRAPHY: Jacob Bean, "Genoese Baroque Drawings" review, *Master Drawings* XI, no. 3, 1973, p. 294, pl. 41; Mary Newcome, "Et nos cedamus Amori: A drawing by Gregorio de Ferrari for the Palazzo Balbi-Senarega," *Bulletin, Allen Memorial Art Museum, Oberlin College* XXI, no. 2, 1973–74, pp. 82–83
The Elisha Whittelsey Collection, The Elisha Whittelsey Fund, 55.628.8

Before coming to Genoa, the city which became his home and which he greatly enriched with his art, Gregorio de Ferrari immersed himself in the works of Correggio in Parma, where he lived for several years. It is often noted that his study of Correggio was decisive for his development of an exuberant lyricism, bravura effects of light and color, and sweeping, rhythmic compositions. These qualities identify the author of this formerly anonymous drawing as Gregorio.

Mary Newcome pointed out the close similarity of the scheme of the architectural ornament in our drawing to that in a drawing in the Palazzo Rosso, Genoa, representing the Assumption of the Virgin (inv. no. 2130, also pen and brown ink on blue gray paper. See E. Gavazza, "Contributo a Gregorio de Ferrari," *Arte antica e moderna* VI, no. 24, p. 330, pl. 135a). According to Gavazza, the Palazzo Rosso drawing is probably for the frescoed vault of the destroyed Genoese church of SS. Giacomo e Filippo. The scheme of this drawing does not, however, conform exactly to descriptions of the church (R. Soprani and C. G. Ratti, *Delle Vite de' Pittori, Scultori, ed Architetti Genovesi,* II, Genoa, 1769, p. 115). Newcome suggested that our drawing was an alternative to the Palazzo Rosso drawing or that both drawings were for a series of chapels.

Gregorio is known mainly for his figure painting, but in Soprani-Ratti he is specifically mentioned in reference to the SS. Giacomo e Filippo frescoes as the designer of the architectural perspective (the *quadratura*) for the vault. Many of his drawings of architectural decoration exist, the most brilliant example of which is now in Oberlin (see Newcome, "Et nos cedamus Amori"). This drawing, formerly in the N. Peretti collection, Rome, was one of the star attractions of the 1972 Binghamton exhibition arranged by Mary Newcome (*Genoese Baroque Drawings,* Binghamton, N.Y., no. 94, repr.).

GIOVANNI BATTISTA FOGGINI
(Florence 1652–1725 Florence)

23a and b Designs for urns supported by a satyr and satyress

(a) Pen, brown ink, with brown wash, over traces of black chalk. 7⅜ x 4½ in. (187 x 114 mm). Partially laid down on paper with a Gothic A stamped in purple ink at lower left corner
Inscribed in brown ink at upper left corner, *S B*

(b) Pen, brown ink, with brown wash, over traces of black chalk. 7⅝ x 4¼ in. (194 x 108 mm). Partially laid down on paper with a Gothic A stamped in purple ink at lower right corner

PROVENANCE: Janos Scholz, New York
The Elisha Whittelsey Collection, The Elisha Whittelsey Fund, 52.570.277,278

During the last half century of Medici rule in Florence before foreign domination, Giovanni Battista Foggini may be said to have ruled in the artistic realm. Foggini studied in Rome from 1673 to 1676 at the newly-founded Florentine Academy. He was greatly influenced there by Roman baroque art and by his teachers: in sculpture, Ercole Ferrata and in drawing, Ciro Ferri, Pietro da Cortona's most gifted assistant. Foggini became *Primo Scultore della Casa Serenissima* in Florence in 1678. In 1694 or early 1695, he was granted the title *Architetto Primario* by Grand Duke Cosimo III de' Medici. These were the "two most important artistic court appointments" in Florence, according to K. Lankheit (in Detroit-Florence, 1974, p. 22). Foggini was close to Grand Duke Cosimo and served him in an even more encompassing fashion than his two titles indicate; for instance, the *Architetto Primario* was in charge of the grand ducal workshops, and therefore of designing all the decorative arts, jewelry, furniture, and other appurtenances for the court.

The most prominent examples of Foggini's work in Florence are the dazzling, silver, high altar for SS. Annunziata (1680–82), the marble reliefs for the Corsini Chapel in S. Maria del Carmine (1683–87), and the relief sculpture, finished in 1692, in the Feroni Chapel, also in SS. Annunziata. The variety of Foggini's *œuvre* may be seen in

the Palazzo Pitti where many of the smaller objects he designed are preserved: a prie-dieu, reliquaries, furniture, and small bronzes.

In the Gabinetto dei Disegni in the Uffizi is a vellum-bound volume of his drawings known by the title on its cover, *Giornale del Foggini* (inv. no. 8027A). The *Giornale,* published by Lankheit (Lankheit, 1959, pp. 55–108; discussed further by Lankheit in 1962 in *Florentinische Barockplastik,* Munich), contains studies for many of Foggini's executed works, architectural and sculptural as well as decorative. Although drawings by Foggini are dispersed throughout many European and some American collections (see for example, those published in Detroit-Florence, 1974), it is in the *Giornale,* containing 170 leaves, many with drawings on the verso, that Foggini's many talents are most completely exhibited.

Foggini's drawings in the Metropolitan number over sixty, of which very few are by his workshop. Most were identified by Rudolf Berliner. Ours is probably the largest collection of his drawings outside Italy. The majority of our drawings are similar both in format and subject to the Uffizi's *Giornale,* with the exception of several large sheets by Foggini in the Museum's Department of Drawings (J. Bean and F. Stampfle, *Drawings from New York Collections, II: The 17th Century in Italy,* New York, 1967, no. 136, repr.; Detroit-Florence, 1974, no. 22, repr.). Many of our Foggini drawings are about the same size as the leaves in the *Giornale* and like them are creased vertically at the center. Some sheets are numbered and set off by a circular penstroke in the upper right corners; for example, No. 27 recto has the circular stroke, and the beginnings of a number can be seen, though it is mostly cut away. The *Giornale* sheets are also numbered in the upper right corners with a circular penstroke to set them off. Many of the drawings in our collection are very small, some as small as two inches square, and must have been cut from larger sheets. It is clear that our larger sheets, those creased vertically, come from a volume like the *Giornale,* and it is probable that the smaller drawings were also originally from a leaf of a book. Most of our drawings were acquired from Janos Scholz, and of these, many are inscribed in the same eighteenth-century hand in brown ink, with the letters *S B.* It is assumed that these letters are the initials of a former owner, but they have not yet been identified.

These designs for vases were no doubt to be executed in bronze. The satyrs and satyresses are favorite themes of Foggini: similar satyrs are supports for clocks on leaves 91 verso and 92 and 93 rectos in the *Giornale* (leaf 92 repr. in Lankheit, 1959, p. 75, fig. 20). Remarkably close to our satyrs are those in a brilliant study for a bronze group in which the satyrs support Bacchus (Uffizi inv. no. 15361F). Other similar studies are on Uffizi sheets inv. nos. 15360F, 15362F, 2803S.

24 Design for a ewer

Pen, brown ink, with brown and gray wash, over black chalk.
10⅞ x 6⅞ in. (276 x 175 mm)
Inscribed in brown ink at upper left, *S B*

PROVENANCE: Janos Scholz, New York
The Elisha Whittelsey Collection, The Elisha Whittelsey
Fund, 52.570.247

Foggini's draughtsmanship is brilliantly exhibited in this
ornate and lively design for a bronze ewer, representing
the Triumph of Neptune. Tritons support the vessel, on
which Neptune, riding two seahorses, is surrounded by
more horn-blowing tritons. A winged siren with a long,
curling tail forms the handle.

A pair of bronze ewers in the Victoria and Albert Museum by Massimiliano Soldani Benzi, Foggini's near contemporary, are strikingly similar to our drawing in their
exuberantly baroque, almost rococo effect (Lankheit, *Florentinische Barockplastik,* pp. 146–148, figs. 146–151; Detroit-Florence, 1974, nos. 84 A, B, repr.). One of the pair
also has Neptune as its subject.

25 Designs for a catafalque with alternative suggestions

Pen, brown ink, over black chalk. 11⅝ x 8⅜ in.
(295 x 213 mm). Vertical crease at center. Some tears and
staining. Watermark: lamb, near Heawood 2835
(ours lacks the inscribing circle)
Verso: Design for catafalque
Pen, brown ink, with traces of gray wash, over black chalk
The Elisha Whittelsey Collection, The Elisha Whittelsey
Fund, 49.63.279

The catafalque designs on both the recto and verso of this
sheet, though compositionally unrelated to each other, are
each similar to ones in other drawings in our collection and
to certain leaves in the *Giornale*.

On the recto of No. 25 are variant studies of a catafalque, decorated with many candles, whose main component is an obelisk in the center of flights of stairs. It
appears in a similar form at the upper right of No. 26
verso. A different design for a complete catafalque is depicted on No. 26 recto and on the verso of No. 25. These
two catafalques have no obelisk; their central feature is
instead an arch supporting the casket on which kneels a
female figure, surmounted by a royal crown. In both Nos.
25 verso and 26 recto, female Virtues sit on balustrades; it
is possible to identify Justice and Faith in No. 26 recto.
No. 25 recto has, in contrast, a male figure seated on the
balustrade of the catafalque.

The obelisk catafalques shown in Nos. 25 recto and
26 verso are similar to still another of our drawings, No.
27 recto. Here, there are no elaborate stairs with balus-

trades, and candles are only suggested in black chalk at the
far right, although the motif of an oval medallion on the
face of the central obelisk conforms to the study at the
lower right of No. 25 recto. In addition, the obelisk in
No. 27 recto is supported by an arch, as is the catafalque
at the upper right of No. 25 recto. In No. 27 recto two
Virtues—Fortitude (?) and Prudence—sit on either side
of the archway. The obelisk theme is repeated by two
smaller obelisks flanking the stairs.

There are several designs for catafalques in the *Giornale*.
Lankheit argued convincingly that one was for the Elector
Palatine Johann Wilhelm of the house of Wittelsbach,
who died in 1716. He was the husband of Grand Duke
Cosimo's only daughter, Anna Maria Luisa, and was his
dear friend and staunchest political ally. On leaf 136 verso
of the *Giornale* (Lankheit, 1959, p. 67, fig. 11) is a catafalque with a central obelisk supported by two lions. The
lions, symbol of the Wittelsbach family, as well as another
sheet in the *Giornale* that is dated 1715, support Lankheit's
identification of this catafalque. Two other leaves in the
Giornale—leaf 147 and leaf 148—also depict catafalques.
Leaf 147 has an arrangement similar to our No. 27 recto
(Lankheit, 1959, p. 68, fig. 12). In it, a lightly sketched
obelisk surmounts a structure with candles over a casket
that has a royal crown. This apparatus sits on a platform at
the sides of which are other obelisks, while two Virtues sit
on socles at the sides of the stairs. Leaf 148 is a partially-
sketched variant of leaf 147 showing the central structure
and omitting the obelisk. Lankheit believed that all three
catafalque designs are connected with the death of the
elector palatine. If so, the similarity between these three
Giornale leaves, especially 147 and 148, and our Nos. 25
recto and 26 verso, as well as between leaf 136 verso and
our No. 27 recto, suggest that our drawings may be connected to Johann Wilhelm.

However, as previously noted, there are two designs for
a distinctly different catafalque on the other sides of Nos.
26 and 27 that commemorate someone other than Johann
Wilhelm. Their distinctive feature is the female figure
above the casket. The crown surmounting the catafalque
is similar to the Tuscan crown after it gained the royal bar
in 1691 when the emperor granted Cosimo his royal title.
I believe one should read the sketchy lines in the center of
the crown in both of our drawings as the Florentine lily
that is the central element of the Tuscan crown. The only
female members of the house of Medici to die while Foggini was active were Cosimo's beloved and revered mother,
Vittoria della Rovere, in 1694, and his estranged and bit-
terly disliked wife, Margherita Luisa d'Orleans, who died
in France in 1721. Vittoria's funeral was celebrated with
appropriate pomp in S. Lorenzo (see D. Moreni, *Conti-
nuazione delle Memorie Istoriche . . . di S. Lorenzo . . . ,*
II, Florence, 1817, p. 63). Moreni gave Vittoria's death as

1693, but all subsequent authors, including Acton, gave it as 1694. Moreni did not describe the funeral decorations or say who designed them. Since Margherita Luisa died away from Florence and was buried in France, Cosimo need not have given her a funeral, but merely a *Te Deum*. However, Cosimo arranged obsequies complete with the usual pomp, including a catafalque, but showed his true feelings in not bothering to attend (H. Acton, *The Last Medici,* London, 1932, p. 302). Margherita Luisa's catafalque is also undescribed.

There are chronological problems if Nos. 25 recto and 26 verso are connected with Vittoria della Rovere and the reverse sides of those sheets with the Elector Johann Wilhelm; the former died in 1694, the latter twenty-two years later. Even if the Medici catafalques commemorate Margherita Luisa, there is still a five-year variance between the catafalque drawings on recto and verso of the same sheet. However, I am not entirely convinced that all three of the *Giornale* sheets are for Johann Wilhelm's catafalque. Leaves 147 and 148 lack the specific Wittelsbach allusion of the lions, and as I have noted, the *Giornale* sheets are close to our Nos. 25 recto, 26 verso (both of which have the same watermark), and perhaps 27 recto. If so, then those drawings, both ours and *Giornale* leaves 147 and 148, remain unidentified, strengthening the case for the connection of the catafalques on the reverse sides to Vittoria delle Rovere or Margherita Luisa.

Catafalques, unless identified by an inscription or specific allusion, are extremely difficult, if not virtually impossible, to identify. Another difficulty is that the architectural components for catafalques were used over and over in varying combinations by their designers, so that what appear to be studies for the same project because of similar motifs may be designs for entirely unrelated ones.

26 Design for a catafalque

Pen, brown ink, with gray wash, over black chalk.
11⅜ x 8¼ in. (289 x 210 mm). Vertical crease at center.
Creased, with small patches of paper pasted at upper left and lower right corners. Watermark: lamb, near Heawood 2835
Verso: Designs for table, niche and catafalque
Pen and brown ink

PROVENANCE: Janos Scholz, New York
The Elisha Whittelsey Collection, The Elisha Whittelsey Fund, 52.570.285

For a discussion of the catafalques on both the recto and verso, see No. 25.

The variant designs for a table whose components are seen both in elevation of the base and in a view of the top, indicate the rich and elaborate style that was the Florentine late baroque. The table top would have been executed in *pietre dure,* inlaid semiprecious stones, a Florentine spe-

cialty. The use of a siren as a table support is not peculiar to Foggini but a traditional seventeenth-century motif. A table in the Uffizi employs the motif of a siren whose form and treatment are very similar to the one in the center sketch of our sheet. The Uffizi table is associated with the Florentine designer Giacinto Maria Marmi (latter half of the seventeenth century, last documented in 1697; see Detroit-Florence, 1974, no. 223, repr.) on the basis of a drawing of a similar siren used as a table support.

It should be noted that there are offprints from other ink drawings on both recto and verso that would only be possible if the drawings were placed next to each other when the ink was still wet. This indicates that the drawings were made in a volume similar to the *Giornale.*

27 Design for a catafalque

Pen, brown ink, over black chalk. 11¾ x 7⅞ in.
(298 x 200 mm). Vertical crease at center. Watermark: three monticules surmounted by a cross and supported on the letters *A* and *B*
Verso: Designs for bed alcoves
Inscribed in pencil vertically at lower right, *No. 21*

PROVENANCE: Giovanni Morelli, Milan and Bergamo, his mark, verso, at lower right (Lugt 1902)
The Elisha Whittelsey Collection, The Elisha Whittelsey Fund, 49.50.112

For a discussion of the catafalque on the recto, see No. 25.

Though acquired at different times and from different sources, both this drawing and No. 28 come from the collection of the art historian and connoisseur, Giovanni Morelli. Both are numbered consecutively in pencil in the same hand; No. 27 is inscribed *No. 21* on the verso, and No. 28 is inscribed *No. 22* on the recto. Although they conform to the sketchbook format, both having vertical creases and offprints, the offprints on No. 27 do not match what would have caused them had it faced No. 28. The penciled numbers were probably made by a former owner, perhaps Morelli himself. However, because of the similarity of motifs, especially the offprint of a doorway with elaborate overdoor decorations, to those on the recto of No. 28, it is likely that they came from the same volume. In addition, the similarity of this catafalque to those in Nos. 25 and 26, and the fact that No. 28 has the same watermark as Nos. 25 and 26, strongly suggest they were once bound together.

As *Architetto Primario* Foggini was both architect and designer. It was in the latter capacity that he made these studies for bed alcoves to be executed, probably in gilt wood, in the grand ducal workshops. The Medici arms in the design at the upper right indicate that they were for one of the Medici palaces or villas. Surmounting the escutcheon in that design is a sketchy crown with a royal bar, thus dating the drawing after 1691. Fantastic creatures are integral parts of the design, as were the siren table supports in No. 26. Here, in the designs at the upper right and at the bottom, winged sirens support the upper wall. Other Foggini motifs are the putti with garlands, and the energetic, intertwining foliage.

There are other small designs among our Foggini drawings that seem to be for similar projects. Two small drawings (acc. nos. 52.570.259, 260) are caryatid supports that are similar to the two isolated studies at the top and bottom of this sheet. On another small drawing is an escutcheon with the Medici arms surmounted by a royal crown (acc. no. 52.570.229; see last page of illustrations), which clearly depicts what is indistinct on this sheet. These three small drawings were probably cut from larger sheets. In a large drawing not by Foggini, but certainly from his workshop, is a finished version of our sketchy alcove entrances (acc. no. 49.62.22). It incorporates many of the elements seen in all our sketches: like the sketch in the center row, right, the escutcheon supporting an unmistakable royal Tuscan crown is enveloped in dense foliage within a semicircle surmounted by an oval cartouche. The putti holding garlands surrounding the escutcheon are closer to those in the sketch at center left. The supports are similar to those in the latter sketch and the freestanding examples.

There is, in addition, another small design by Foggini in the Museum's collection for an alcove entrance with similar fantastic designs (acc. no. 52.570.231). This drawing is very closely related to a drawing by Foggini recently on the London art market. In the London drawing the bed in its alcove is very clearly drawn, and shows that the two bottom sketches in No. 27 of a bed surmounted by a crown-baldachino were to be placed behind the alcove wall divisions represented in the upper four sketches. The flowers in the crown-baldachino on our sheet can be identified as lilies, another allusion to the Medici and Florence.

28 Designs for chapels and portals

Pen, brown ink, with gray wash, over black chalk.
11⅝ x 8⅛ in. (295 x 206 mm). Vertical crease at center.
Watermark: lamb, near Heawood 2835
Inscribed in pencil at lower left, *No. 22*
Verso: Designs for altars and urns

PROVENANCE: Giovanni Morelli, Milan and Bergamo, his mark, verso, at lower right (Lugt 1902)
Gift of Janet S. Byrne, 52.591

This drawing comes from the same collection as No. 27, and its provenance is discussed there.

The inclusion on one leaf of such diverse designs as architecture, chapels, altars, decorative objects, and urns, is characteristic of many leaves in the *Giornale*. The chapels

on the recto demonstrate Foggini's precise and careful draughtsmanship in his purely architectural studies. A similarly restrained design is on leaf 121 of the *Giornale* (Lankheit, 1959, fig. 24). The first pages of the *Giornale* contain altar designs (leaves 5–11; see Lankheit, 1959, p. 93) in which the series is interrupted on leaf 8 verso by a decorated vase. Foggini was charged with the designs for many chapels, some in private palaces. The designs on the recto are unidentified as they do not conform to any of his well-known, published chapels.

At the top of the verso are four designs for an altar with an arched top. A figure with arm outstretched is repeated at the side of the two left altars. The altar at center right seems unrelated to the other four since it is crowned by a double pediment. Represented within the altar frame is the Baptism of Christ with God the Father in a glory with putti above. Similar studies for the figures of Christ and John the Baptist are on the verso of another drawing in our collection (acc. no. 52.570.242). Like No. 28, this sheet depicts a decorative object: in this case a reliquary. At the lower left of that sheet is a study for the figure of Christ kneeling with arms crossed over his chest, with the Baptist at the right, a staff held in his bent left arm, and his right extended toward Christ. A study of the Baptist alone, viewed more frontally, is in the lower right corner. There are striking similarities between the altar study in No. 28 verso and a bronze group in the Seattle Art Museum (Detroit-Florence, 1974, no. 13, repr.) depicting the Baptism, made in 1723 by Foggini for Cosimo's daughter, the electress palatine. The unidentified rounded vessel in the Baptist's right hand in our drawing is a shell in the bronze. The Baptism in 28 verso within an altar was planned for sculpture in very high relief or in the round. Because of its altar context, this drawing should probably not be dated to the same date as the bronze. Presumably Foggini had the sketch on hand and reused it when designing the bronze. However, this suggests a late date for the drawing. If this drawing is, indeed, from the same sketchbook as No. 27, whose catafalque is probably related to those in Nos. 25 and 26, then a stronger case is made for the connection of the catafalques in Nos. 25 verso and 26 recto with the funeral of Margherita Luisa in 1721.

The nine urns to be executed in silver reveal Foggini's imagination in the treatment of a theme. While the basic shape remains the same, there is rich variation in the handles that are formed of satyrs, lions, sirens, putti, and foliage. A similar but more distinctly drawn urn is depicted on leaf 57 of the *Giornale*. This urn, and thus also those on No. 28 verso, were to be coffee urns, *caffetiere*, as seen by the spouts issuing from the masks at the base of the vessels.

The interrelationship among Nos. 25–28 and many sheets in the *Giornale* suggests the possibility that our drawings are some of the missing sheets from the *Giornale*.

CARLO FONTANA
(Bruciate near Como 1638–1714 Rome)

29 Design for the façade of SS. Faustino e Giovita, Rome

Pen, brown ink, with brown and gray wash, over black chalk; the background in faint red wash; brown ink border on drawing. 22⁹⁄₁₆ x 14⅝ in. (574 x 372 mm). Some tears, repaired. Foxed. Alternate scheme on hinged paper flap over doorway. Watermark: kneeling man holding a baton, near C. M. Briquet, *Les Filigranes,* II, 2nd ed., Leipzig, 1923, 7628, 7629
Signed in brown ink within drawing at lower right, *C Fontana*

BIBLIOGRAPHY: H. Hager, "Le Facciate dei SS. Faustino e Giovita e di S. Biagio in Campitelli (S. Rita) a Roma: A Proposito di due Opere giovanili di Carlo Fontana," *Commentari* XXIII, no. 111, 1972, pp. 261–271
The Elisha Whittelsey Collection, The Elisha Whittelsey Fund, 61.658.39

In the last decade of the seventeenth century, Carlo Fontana became surveyor of St. Peter's and was also elected president of the Accademia di S. Luca for a second term, an honor which Wittkower described as "a mark of esteem without precedent." Thus as the new century opened, he was Rome's most eminent architect, the one with the greatest number and variety of official commissions. His classicizing architecture was characterized by its clarity and precision, while his chapels, often richly ornamented, were quietly elegant. This became the prevailing official style in Rome during the first two decades of the eighteenth century. Just as he was inspired by Bernini, in whose studio he worked from 1656, Fontana greatly influenced his own pupils and assistants—the most notable of whom was Juvarra—with his special brand of cool, academic classicism. Some of Fontana's most interesting and beautiful works are the curved façade of S. Marcello al Corso (1682–83), the Cibò Chapel in S. Maria del Popolo (1683–87), and one of his earliest, S. Biagio in Campitelli.

He is represented here by a design for the façade of the small Roman church of SS. Faustino e Giovita (1664), an early work contemporary with S. Biagio with which it has a number of features in common. SS. Faustino e Giovita, originally on Via Giulia, was destroyed in 1890 in the regularization of the Tiber and the Lungotevere. The drawing was identified and published by H. Hager ("Le Facciate," p. 262, figs. 1, 2), who discussed SS. Faustino e Giovita in relation to the much better known and still extant S. Biagio. Both churches were small, with two-storied façades divided into three bays, and both shared the same motif: a pediment that does not crown the entire width of the façade, but only the central portion. The façade of SS. Faustino e Giovita as executed is known through an engraving by Matteo Gregorio de Rossi (ibid., p. 264, fig. 4). Its most striking feature is the treatment of that crowning

pediment. Within the triangle of the pediment is placed a conch-shell-shaped oval which is enlarged beyond the field of the triangle, extending down to the top of the arched window.

The Metropolitan drawing differs from the final façade primarily in the central doorway, which the engraving shows as having a conventionally classical triangular pediment. A drawing for the façade in the Ashmolean Museum, Oxford (Large Talman Album, fol. 10; ibid., p. 263, fig. 3) presents this doorway, as well as a plain frieze above it (whereas the Metropolitan drawing has a frieze containing triglyphs, an unusual motif on Roman façades, as Hager noted). The Ashmolean drawing is thus the basis for the execution of the building, and the Metropolitan sheet an earlier study.

The Metropolitan design shows Fontana considering an unconventional motif for the doorway. A flap of paper pasted over the central portal in the Metropolitan version presents an alternate suggestion to the first one underneath. The first idea for the portal was an oval in a medallion, echoing Fontana's distinctive upper pediment. This solution was replaced by the essentially boring one offered on the flap over the drawing: a plain, enlarged rectangular doorway. The solution for the portal with its repetition of the triangular pediment, as seen in both the Ashmolean drawing and the engraving, was a more restrained and balanced design.

Although the precise chronological sequence between SS. Faustino e Giovita and S. Biagio has not been determined, it is known that they are nearly contemporary. At about the same time that Fontana opted for a basically classical and conservative design for SS. Faustino e Giovita, he detached himself from that tradition in the design of the architecturally more adventuresome and interesting church of S. Biagio in Campitelli, his first artistically independent and truly distinguished work.

DONATO GIUSEPPE FRISONI
(Laino near Como 1683–1735 Ludwigsburg)

30 Design for the salon of the pleasure pavilion, Favorita, at Ludwigsburg, 1718

Pen, brown, and gray ink, with gray, rose, and yellow green wash, heightened with gold; brown ink border on drawing. 19½ x 25⅜ in. (495 x 645 mm). Vertical crease at center. Some tears, repaired
Inscribed in brown ink at lower left, *Eberhard Ludwig Hz;* at right of that in gray ink, *profillo della Salla dalla favorita nel Giardino de fasani per la Sua Altza Sema il Semo di Wirtinberg a Louisbourg per farsi di spechij et stucho la soffitta dipinta a fresco;* signed in gray ink at lower right with part of date obscured, *D. G. Frisoni 1[7]18*

PROVENANCE: Leon Dalva, New York, Piedmontese scrapbook
Gift of Leon Dalva, 65.654.1

This drawing comes from a large scrapbook of unknown provenance containing drawings mainly Piedmontese in origin: many have scales in the Piedmontese measurements of *trabucchi* and *piedi liprandi*. Some of the drawings were for the decoration of the royal palace at Moncalieri, near Turin, by Leonardo Marini (Nos. 40–42). The style of architectural decoration in Lombardy near the Piedmontese border and in the section around Como and the lakes derives essentially from that developed in Piedmont. It therefore must have seemed consistent to the album's original owner to include this drawing of a German project by a native of a town between Lakes Como and Lugano. This is not to say, however, that the ornament in this drawing is wholly in this Piedmontese-Lombard style. Although nothing seems to be known of Frisoni's earliest work, it was probably in the provincial style of his region. It was then modified by his early residence in Prague (1707–09) where, as a stucco designer, or *stuccatore,* in the Sternberg Palace, he would have come into contact with a Viennese proto-rococo style.

In 1709 he was called from Prague to work at the great palace at Ludwigsburg near Stuttgart, by its chief architect, J. F. Nette, who had planned the enormous complex for the duke of Württemberg, Eberhard Ludwig (1676–1733). Frisoni, beginning there as a *stuccatore,* rose rapidly, soon became one of Nette's major assistants, and finally in 1715, was made chief architect, following Nette's sudden death the year before (S. Fleischhauer, *Barock in Herzogtum Württemberg,* Stuttgart, 1958, p. 178). The central core of the palace had already been erected on Nette's plan, but Frisoni enlarged it and began to design the complex gardens and out-buildings, one of which was the Favorita, a pleasure pavilion erected in 1718–19 by P. Retti on Frisoni's design. Its position in a pheasant garden on a wooded hill that rises behind the palace can be seen in the engraving from the sumptuous early eighteenth-century book, *Vües de la Residence Ducale de Louisbourg* (Augsburg, n.d.). Unfortunately, the book has no engraving of the interior of the *salone* of the Favorita, since Frisoni's original decorations were pulled down to be replaced by the dry and uninspired neoclassic ones seen there today. Only the side rooms retain the original decoration (see Fleischhauer, *Barock,* fig. 160). The Metropolitan drawing is an especially precious document as it records the original decorations now lost. That this is not merely one of a series of studies for the decoration of the *salone* is illustrated by the nearly undecipherable signature of approval of Duke Eberhard Ludwig that appears on the drawing (for other contract drawings approved by the duke, see ibid., fig. 125).

The splendor of the mirrored and stuccoed room, inlaid with marble and heightened with gilded interlaced bandwork, stands out in this ornate drawing. Only the frescoes to be painted on the ceiling, alluded to in the inscription, are lacking. The figures seated on the mantlepieces personify Architecture, Sculpture, Painting, and Music. Allusions to the duke are in the intertwined letters *E* and *L* decorating the firebacks, to the palace in the *L*s on the doors at the left, and to the duchy of Württemberg in the *W*s on the doors at the right.

FABRIZIO GALLIARI
(Andorno 1709–1790 Treviglio)

31 RECTO:
Design for a stage set: a courtyard

Pen, brown ink, with gray wash. 8 x 10⅝16 in. (203 x 262 mm). Inlaid into modern paper
Inscribed in pencil at lower left, *Piranesi*

BERNARDINO GALLIARI
(Andorno 1707–1794 Andorno)

31 VERSO:
Design for a stage set: a landscape

Brush, brown ink, over traces of graphite
PROVENANCE: S. Kaufman, London
EXHIBITIONS: Portsmouth, 1969, no. 53, repr.
Harris Brisbane Dick Fund and Joseph Pulitzer Bequest, 1971.513.65

The closeness with which families of stage designers worked is demonstrated by this sheet which combines on the recto and verso drawings by the two Galliari brothers. The identification was made by Mercedes Viale Ferrero (cited in Portsmouth, 1969, no. 53; see also Viale Ferrero, *La Scenografia del '700 e i fratelli Galliari,* Turin, 1963). The two brothers collaborated closely in Turin as well as in Milan where they dominated theatrical design. They worked also in other North Italian towns and, like the Bibienas, in Austria as well. The many descendants of the Galliari brothers were active in stage design through the first quarter of the eighteenth century.

According to Viale Ferrero, these sets were possibly designed for the opera *Mitridate* given in Turin at the Teatro Regio in 1767. The recto may be for scene 8, act 3, described as a large courtyard with arcades, and the verso, scene 5, act 2, the encampment of Mitridate near the bank of a river (see Viale Ferrero, *La Scenografia del '700,* p. 45, figs. 68, 69). Kaufman and Knox mentioned in the Portsmouth catalogue that the size of the sheet approximates one from an album and suggested that this sheet might be one of the many sheets missing from a Galliari album in the Pinacoteca at Bologna (Album XII) that contains other drawings for *Mitridate.*

The Metropolitan possesses a study by Fabrizio for a set identified as *Appartimenti Reali* for the opera *Ifigenia,* which was performed at the Teatro Regio, Turin, in 1762 (ibid., pp. 84, 249, 252, 273, with related drawings).

LUIGI GARZI
(Pistoia 1638–1721 Rome)

32 Design for a painted wall decoration

Pen, brown ink, with gray wash. 11 x 15 in. (286 x 381 mm)
Inscribed in brown ink at lower left, *uigi Garzi le 8 Decembre 1708*
Gift of Charles B. Wrightsman, 1970.736.49

Garzi came as a young man to Rome, was a pupil of Andrea Sacchi, and enjoyed success decorating palaces and designing altars and church ceilings throughout Rome. He was a member of the Accademia di S. Luca and the Virtuosi del Pantheon.

This drawing is a pendant to another in the Metropolitan (acc. no. 1970.736.48) in which Garzi copied a drawing now at Christ Church, Oxford (no. D77), for Pietro da Cortona's decorations for the now-transformed Galleria Alessandro VII in the Quirinal Palace (1656–57). N. Wirbiral discussed this project ("Contributi alle Ricerche sul Cortonismo in Roma: I Pittori della Galleria di Alessandro VII del Palazzo del Quirinale," *Bolletino d'Arte* LII, 1960, pp. 123–165), and Sabine Jacob added further information ("Pierre de Cortone et la décoration de la Galerie d'Alexandre VII au Quirinal," *Revue de l'Art,* no. 11, 1971, pp. 42–54). In his article, Wirbiral wrongly attributed the Christ Church drawing to G. F. Grimaldi. Jacob corrected this, attributing the drawing to Cortona's atelier, while James Byam Shaw sustained the traditional attribution to Cortona himself (*Old Master Drawings from Christ Church, Oxford* [exhibition catalogue], International Exhibitions Foundation, 1972–73, no. 21, repr.). Both of the Metropolitan's Garzi drawings, in addition to two more recently on the London art market, record one stage of Cortona's intended decoration for the Galleria.

A drawing in the Kunstmuseum, Düsseldorf (inv. no. FP 8070; Jacob, "Pierre de Cortone," p. 43, fig. 3, as Cortona's atelier) is a preliminary sketch for the wall, including the section which this Garzi drawing fully elaborates. Jacob sees this scheme as a first stage in the development of Cortona's final design as it is known, she says, through a drawing in the Kunstbibliothek, Berlin (Hdz 879; ibid., p. 44, fig. 4) in which the frames above the doors are simplified to plain rectangles, the figures in front of the columns between the doorways are eliminated, and the decoration above the door frame is changed to volutes on either side of a cartouche containing the Chigi *monti.*

The French spelling of the date on our drawing is puzzling. It has been conjectured that the drawing was commissioned by a French patron.

FELICE GIANI
(S. Sebastiano di Monferrato near Genoa 1758–1823 Rome)

33a and b Designs for a palace interior

(a) Interior of a palace, elevation and ceiling
Pen, brown ink, with blue, rose, yellow, and green wash. 11⅝ x 8 in. (295 x 203 mm). Gothic A stamped in purple ink at lower left
Inscribed in brown ink at bottom, *Gabinetto quarto canto Virgilio*

(b) Ceiling of a palace
Pen, brown ink, with colored wash. 8 x 10¼ in. (203 x 260 mm)
Inscribed in brown ink at bottom, *Camera da ricever canto sesto Virgilio*

PROVENANCE: Janos Scholz, New York
The Elisha Whittelsey Collection, The Elisha Whittelsey Fund, 52.570.64, 65

Giani was one of the foremost decorative painters of his time. He obtained a thorough foundation in his field as pupil of Antonio Bibiena in Pavia, and then in 1778, of the painter Ubaldo Gandolfi in Bologna. In Rome by 1780, he studied both at the Accademia di S. Luca and with Pompeo Batoni.

In 1786 he was briefly in Faenza and returned there in 1794. For the next eighteen years he worked out of Faenza. He was active in Ferrara, Forlì, Ravenna, and Bologna, and made trips to Milan, Naples, Rimini, Venice, and Montmorency. His visit to Paris in 1803 led to the spread of his personal, romantic brand of neoclassicism that greatly contributed to the French Empire style. His most important work in Paris was the decoration of the Tuileries Palace, now destroyed, for Napoleon. His last years were spent in Rome and were capped by the official honors of election to the Accademia di S. Luca in 1811 and of membership in the Roman Congregazione dei Virtuosi del Pantheon in 1819. Of the large number of his drawings that were in the Giovanni Piancastelli collection, Rome, many are now in the Cooper-Hewitt Museum and in the Biblioteca and Museo Civico di Faenza. Several of his drawings are in the Musée des Arts Décoratifs, Paris.

The exhibited drawings were first identified by Rudolf Berliner, who also identified as by Giani a group of drawings in the Musée des Arts Décoratifs, among which are some with scales in *piedi di Faenza* and *piedi di Forlì.* These ceiling designs are similar to ours, and have similar inscriptions identifying the subjects as from Virgil's *Aeneid.* Giani's free and graceful evocation of classical Roman decoration is evident in our drawing, which may be for one of his many room decorations for palaces in Faenza. For example, in 1817–18, he decorated rooms depicting scenes from the *Aeneid* in the now-destroyed Palazzo Pasolini dall' Onda, with the assistance of Gaetano Bertolani (A. Montanari, *Guida Storica di Faenza,* Faenza, 1882, p. 169; further on Giani's decoration in Faenza, E. Golfieri, *La casa faentina dell' Ottocento, I: Architettura e decorazioni,* Faenza [1969], unpaged introduction).

The interior of 33a is decorated with scenes from the fourth book of the *Aeneid,* describing Aeneas' liason with Dido, their separation, and her suicide. The reception room depicted in 33b illustrates the sixth book, concerning Aeneas' visit to Hell. The central panel of the ceiling drawing in No. 33b may well represent the meeting of Aeneas and Dido in Hell.

DOMENICO SILVESTRO GIANNOTTI
(Lucca 1680–1750 Bologna)

34 Design for carved mirror frame surmounting a mantle

Pen, brown ink, over black chalk. 12 x 8¼ in.
(305 x 210 mm)
Inscribed in brown ink within the design, *Troumeau sop:ª Cam:ⁿᵒ/ del Giannotti 1742*
The Elisha Whittelsey Collection, The Elisha Whittelsey Fund, 49.63.275

A peripatetic sculptor in wood, designer of intarsia, and silversmith, Giannotti is best known for his works in Bologna, principally the carved anatomical statues for the Teatro Anatomico in the Archiginnasio. He studied in Rome with a minor Bolognese decorative painter, returning in 1700 to his birthplace. It was there that he executed eight silver torcheres for the Cappella del Volto Santo in the cathedral on a design approved by Juvarra (E. Ridolfi, *L'Arte in Lucca. . .* , Lucca, 1882, p. 249). He is documented in towns throughout Emilia. He was back in Rome in 1732. In 1741 he returned again to Lucca where he opened his own school of sculpture as part of the newly formed Accademia di Belle Arti. He made our drawing the following year.

The Museum acquired the drawing with a group by other artists, notably G. B. Natali (Nos. 46, 47), all of which are inscribed by the same eighteenth-century hand, identifying the artists and noting, in some cases, the dates.

It is probable that this attractive mirror frame was designed for the Palazzo Bernardini in Lucca since two of the drawings by Natali in the group carry the arms of that illustrious family. Moreover, Giannotti received a pension from, and was under the protection of, the same Bernardini family (I. Belli Barsali, *Guida di Lucca,* Lucca, 1970, p. 229).

The whole-hearted rococo decoration of this mirror was unusual for its date in Tuscany, where the legacy of Foggini's stately late baroque style still dominated.

GIUSEPPE JARMORINI
(Bologna about 1732–1816 Bologna)

35 Design for a palace façade

Pen, brown ink, with gray wash, over graphite. 10 x 7½ in.
(254 x 191 mm)
Inscribed, verso, in brown ink at lower right, *Jarmorini Giuseppe Bolognese*

PROVENANCE: Sale, Berlin, Galerie G. Bassenge, *Auktion no. 13,* 6–10 May 1969, part I, lot 595
The Elisha Whittelsey Collection, The Elisha Whittelsey Fund, 69.574.1

An architect and painter of *quadratura,* and member of the Accademia Clementina, Jarmorini was a prolific draughtsman. Many of his drawings are in the Cini Foundation and the Graphische Sammlung, Munich. A lesser number are in the Cooper-Hewitt Museum, and some, of course, are in the Accademia di Belle Arti, Bologna, where he studied, winning the prize *Seconda Classe* in 1759 for a design for chapels and a *Prima Classe* in 1761 for the design of a garden wall. Contrary to the usual practice of his contemporaries, he signed many of his drawings, either on the recto, or as here, on the verso.

A drawing by Jarmorini in the Cooper-Hewitt Museum (acc. no. 1938–88–5190) dated 1807 shares some of the architectural features seen here: the segmented obelisk finials surmounting both ends of the pediment and the use of shallow niches for statues. Our drawing is therefore probably to be dated either late in the eighteenth century, or in the first decade of the nineteenth. The restrained sobriety of the façade is typical of Bolognese architecture and contrasts sharply with its interior decoration.

FILIPPO JUVARRA
(Messina 1678–1736 Madrid)

36 Album of drawings

125 leaves bound in vellum, numbered recto and verso in sequence as pages. Inside front cover has blemish 2 x 1⅝ in. (50 x 42 mm) where a bookplate was removed. Drawings on both recto and verso of the leaves in various media: pen, brown ink; pen, brown ink, with brown wash; some with gray wash; most over black chalk, but some sketches only in black chalk; several in red chalk. 11¾ x 8⅜ in. (298 x 213 mm). Most of the leaves are nearly the size of the binding. Some are very much smaller, and two are much larger. Watermarks: see Appendix (page 55)

PROVENANCE: Bartolommeo Sestini, Capoliveri, Elba, formerly Pisa; sale, Sala delle Stagioni, Pisa, 20 May 1966, lot 98 as Filippo Vasconi, two repr.; private collection, London

BIBLIOGRAPHY: Messina, 1966, pp. 10, 43, 44, 116, 117, figs. 223, 224; Andreina Griseri, *Le metamorfosi del Barocco*, Turin, 1967, p. 287; Mercedes Viale Ferrero, *Filippo Juvarra: scenografo e architetto teatrale*, New York and London, 1970, pp. 9, 11, notes 10–12; Hellmut Hager, *Filippo Juvarra e il concorso di modelli del 1715 bandito da Clemente XI per la nuova sacrestia di S. Pietro*, Rome, 1970, p. 53, note 60; Henry A. Millon, "La Formazione Piemontese di B. Vittone fino al 1742," *Bernardo Vittone e la Disputa fra Classicismo e Barocco nel Settecento, Atti del Convegno Internazionale...*, Turin, 1972, p. 453

Rogers Fund, 69.655

Unknown until 1966, this album provides many insights into the early years of the man who became the greatest Italian architect of his time. Filippo Juvarra built at Stupinigi, near Turin, a hunting lodge of unparalleled splendor and delight for Vittorio Amadeo II of Savoy. Many other of his architectural masterpieces grace the city of Turin.

It is clear from the different sizes, formats, and watermarks of the leaves in our volume that it is not a sketchbook, but rather an album composed of sheets already drawn upon and then bound together, most likely by Juvarra himself. He was a prolific draughtsman who delighted in the act of drawing and who took pains to collect many of his drawings together into such albums (see Messina, 1966, p. 107, no. 6, and p. 116; and R. Pommer, *Eighteenth-Century Architecture in Piedmont...*, New York and London, 1967, pp. 139–140). Juvarra had, moreover, the example of his teacher, Carlo Fontana, who at the time that Juvarra was working with him, was gathering his own drawings into volumes (see A. Blunt, "The Drawings of Carlo Fontana in the Royal Library at Windsor Castle," *Congressi salentini I: Barocco europeo, barocco italiano, barocco salentino*, Lecce 1970, pp. 89–92).

A volume in the Biblioteca Nazionale, Turin (Riserva 59–4) is a scrapbook of Juvarra drawings, some from an early sketchbook containing Roman drawings of the same period as ours (see Andreina Griseri, "Itinerari juvarriani," *Paragone* XCIII, 1957, pp. 40–59). Another volume that relates to ours, formerly in the Tournon collection, Turin, contains drawings dated 1706 made in Rome and Naples (this volume has been unavailable for study for several years; see Rovere, Viale, Brinckmann, p. 158; Messina, 1966, p. 110, there designated as private collection, vol. 1).

Our album covers Juvarra's early, pre-Turin career in Messina, Rome, and Lucca. Since the leaves are already numbered like pages, for convenience the drawings will be referred to by these numbers.

The son and brother of silversmiths, Juvarra received, according to his early biographers, no formal training in architecture, but instead studied the treatises of Vitruvius, Vignola, and Pozzo. Juvarra's earliest architectural work was for the church of S. Gregorio in Messina (about 1701–

03; see M. Accascina, "La Formazione Artistica di Filippo Juvarra," *Bollettino d'Arte* XLII, 1957, pp. 152–158; M. Accascina, *Profilo dell' Architettura a Messina dal 1600 al 1800*, Rome, 1964, pp. 95–101) for which we possess several drawings (pp. 127, 192–199). In addition, our album contains other Messina projects, including a design for the *scalone* in the palace of Prince Mario Spadafora (pp. 93–95).

Juvarra arrived in Rome not later than the summer of 1704 and was soon presented to Carlo Fontana. Fontana is reported by one of Juvarra's contemporary biographers, Scipione Maffei, to have told Juvarra, on seeing his drawings, to unlearn everything he already knew, to study the architecture of Michelangelo, and to go and draw the Palazzo Farnese (Messina, 1966, p. 18). Drawings in our volume, as well as one in the former Tournon album (Messina, 1966, p. 43) reveal that Fontana's advice was taken.

The name of Filippo Vasconi appears on the first page of the album. The possibility that Vasconi owned the album has certainly to be considered, although the name was written by Juvarra and the drawing on p. 1, incorporating architectural ideas of Fontana, is certainly his. Vasconi was Fontana's nephew and pupil; although much younger than Juvarra, Vasconi and he were members of the same circle and friends during the years covered by our album. The connection to Vasconi may be because he was a printmaker who later executed etchings for Juvarra; there are several projects for prints in the album. In 1721, Vasconi etched two large sheets depicting Juvarra's Palazzo Madama, Turin, and in the following year he added two plates to Juvarra's book of designs of coats of arms entitled *Raccolta di varie targhe*. Vasconi's name also appears on p. 98 in a list of names that includes Juvarra's.

The drawings chosen for reproduction in this catalogue are those that best exhibit Juvarra's superb draughtsmanship, that relate to executed projects, and that show, like the *targhe* and clock designs, further dimensions of the artist's talents.

For further information on the drawings, see Appendix (p. 55).

36a and b Architectural fantasies

(PAGES 55, 57)

(a) Pen, brown ink, with wash, over black chalk. 9¹⁵/₁₆ in. at right margin, varying to 9¾ in. at left, by 24⅝ in. (252, 248 x 625 mm), composed of two sheets pieced together and folded. Watermark: fleur-de-lys within a circle with an F below

Inscribed, verso, in brown ink, *Pensiero d'un disegnio da farsi/ [ai—?] Sig^re Principale della/ Accademia [—] ideare/ il Campidoglio festanta/ per la si detta*

(b) Pen, brown ink, with wash, over black chalk. 9⅞ in. at right margin, varying to 9⁹⁄₁₆ in. at left, by 22¼ in. (251, 243 x 565 mm), composed of two sheets pieced together and folded
Inscribed, verso, in brown ink, *Altro pensiero per il / Medesimo*

These two drawings, the most beautiful in the album, contain an inscription and other specific allusions to the Accademia di S. Luca such as the name *Joseph Gezzi* on the tablet held by the statue at far right on 36a. Giuseppe Ghezzi was the Perpetual Secretary of the Accademia during Juvarra's early years in Rome. The Accademia met for ceremonial occasions on the Campidoglio, which is depicted here in a highly idealized view from the piazza below, with the Palazzo de' Conservatori and the Palazzo Nuovo partially distinguishable with nets stretched between them. Juvarra's partially illegible inscription does not explain these drawings' specific purpose in relation to the Accademia.

The *tempietto* at left, encircled by a colonnade and set between two pyramids, is surmounted in 36a by an equilateral triangle, which is yet another allusion to the Accademia. In 1705, an equilateral triangle symbolizing the equality of the three arts—Architecture, Sculpture, and Painting—was chosen as the new emblem of the Accademia (M. Missirini, *Memorie per servire alla storia della Romana Accademia di S. Luca...*, Rome, 1823, pp. 170, 171). The triangle itself was formed by the instruments used in these arts: pen, chisel, and compass. Juvarra used this symbol again in two of the four triumphal arches in the album he designed for the Accademia in 1707; on one it is combined with medallions containing the names of the three arts (pp. 79, 81; see Werner Oechslin, "Aspetti dell' internazionalismo nell' architettura italiana del primo Settecento," *Congressi salentini I: Barocco europeo, barocco italiano, barocco salentino*, Lecce, 1970, p. 147, note 8; on later triumphal arches for the Accademia, see W. E. Stopfel, "Triumphbogenentwürfe des 18. Jahrhunderts im Archiv der R. Accademia di S. Luca in Rom," *Kunstgeschichtliche Studien für Kurt Bauch zum 70. Geburtstag...*, Berlin and Munich, 1967, pp. 241–252).

The drawing on 36b, another idea for the same project, as Juvarra noted on the verso, substitutes the Accademia emblem surmounting the *tempietto* with symbols of the arts, of which a palette is the most discernible. The two medallions hanging at the sides and a third out of view in the back may each contain a reference to one of the arts, as was the case on the triumphal arch on p. 81 of our album. The shield held by the statue at left contains sketchy indications of a coat of arms. The X over an open oval at the top of the shield suggests the crossed keys and tiara of the papal arms, while the indication of a band over sketchy lines suggesting monticules is close to the Albani family arms, indicating that these may be the arms of the reigning

pope, Clement XI Albani.

In 1709, members of the Accademia were asked by the pope to prepare views of ancient Rome in honor of the visit of the king of Denmark. Juvarra chose the Campidoglio as his theme, first making two drawings of it as it then appeared (Rovere, Viale, Brinckmann, p. 52, pls. 10–18; Messina, 1966, pp. 49–50, figs. 22–26). However, our drawings do not resemble any of that series very closely, and since they depict the sixteenth-century buildings on the Campidoglio, they are seemingly unrelated to the studies of the Campidoglio in antiquity.

Both 36a and b combine ancient, Renaissance, and baroque motifs. Antiquity is evoked in 36a by the obelisks and by the base of the statue at right, whose garland swags recall an ancient altar, although the shape is a baroque oval. The base of the statue at left recalls Roman funerary monuments. On 36b the urns are additional reminiscences of antiquity. The *tempietto* derived from Bramante recalls the Renaissance, but is treated in a baroque idiom, while the giant order of the curved arcade with engaged half columns inevitably reminds one of Bernini's colonnade at St. Peter's.

Just such a mélange of period motifs occurs in other early Juvarra drawings, in our album (36c, d, and e), and especially those in the former Tournon volume (leaves 106, 107; Rovere, Viale, Brinckmann, pl. 9) and in Riserva 59–4 in the Biblioteca Nazionale, Turin (for example, leaf 20; ibid., pl. 8). Juvarra continued throughout his career to combine architectural styles, in drawings for stage sets as well as in free, architectural sketches such as these.

36c, d, and e Architectural fantasies

(PAGES 13, 97, 63)

(c) Pen, brown ink, over black chalk
Inscribed in brown ink, *Prospettive Fatti a 15: Agosto/ 1704. in Roma*

(d) Pen, brown ink, over black chalk. Watermark: three monticules surmounted by a bird within a circle surmounted by an *F*, near Heawood 166
Inscribed in brown ink, *Prospettive fatte a 28 Agosto in Roma/ L'año 1706*

(e) Black chalk. Watermark: anchor within a circle surmounted by a star over an *F*, near Heawood 5 and 6, but lacking the letters within the circle
Inscribed in brown ink, *Per disegni da rigalare*

The date on 36c, 15 August 1704, makes this drawing not only Juvarra's first dated Roman drawing, but his first dated drawing now known. The drawing sheds some light on the problem of when Juvarra arrived in Rome. Viale and Pommer had thought it to be in late 1703 or early 1704 (Messina, 1966, p. 42; R. Pommer, *Eighteenth-Century Architecture in Piedmont*, p. 23). On 5 May 1705

Juvarra won the architecture prize in the Accademia di S. Luca's Concorso Clementino, which he reportedly entered when it was already in progress, therefore having to prepare his design quickly. Hager suggested that the pressing circumstances ruled out his arrival in Rome before the early autumn of 1704 (H. Hager, *Filippo Juvarra...*, pp. 16, 17, 53, note 53). Our drawing pushes up that date into the summer of 1704.

The monuments in this drawing are all antique, or rather Juvarra's variations on antique monuments. It contains sarcophagi, huge urns, pyramids that recall that of Caius Cestius, and in the monument in the lower sketch, a reconstruction of a mausoleum like that of Hadrian, the Castel S. Angelo. An obelisk lies on the ground. The round colonnaded temple in the upper drawing is modeled on the temple of Vesta, but with differences; for example, never in antiquity would it have contained an obelisk standing within and rising above it. This early Roman drawing testifies to the freshness of his imagination on first viewing Rome and its ancient monuments. The draughtsmanship is striking: Juvarra used a broad pen, drawing quickly and decisively. The style recalls no one so much as Piranesi, and is a remarkable anticipation of his style (on Juvarra and Piranesi, see Griseri, *Le metamorfosi del Barocco*, pp. 293–294).

In the drawing made two years later, 36d, Juvarra played even more freely with antique forms, mixing in baroque elements as well. The scene at left, with a column in front of a church, is reminiscent of Trajan's column and S. Maria di Loreto. The monument in the sketch at right is composed of layered blocks supported by sphinxes, surmounted by an urn, and decorated with garlands. It depends in its essential form on ancient marble candelabra, though radically altered and given baroque flourishes like the broken, segmental pediment, and monumentalized. Juvarra's and Filippo Vasconi's names are listed with others on the verso.

The black chalk sketch, 36e, containing a similar, ancient, candelabrumlike monument seen against a curved colonnade, may have served as a preliminary study for 36d. Its inscription indicates it was meant either as a gift or to be worked up. There are so few Juvarra drawings done only in black chalk, and so many in ink over black chalk underdrawing, that one may assume that this and similar sketches were meant to be worked over with pen and ink.

Still another variation on ancient candelabra appears in a drawing in the former Tournon volume (leaf 107; Rovere, Viale, Brinckmann, pl. 9). It is set next to a colonnade much like that in 36e. Many of the drawings in the former Tournon volume are dated 1706; perhaps they, with ours, were part of a series executed about the same time.

36f and g Designs for a villa

(PAGES 75, 77)

(f) Pen, brown ink, with brown and gray wash, over black chalk. Watermark: anchor within a circle surmounted by a star over an *F*, near Heawood 5 and 6, but lacking the letters within the circle
Inscribed in brown ink, *Palazzina da farsi in Lucca/ vicino a Viareggio* [——]/ *Sig^re Guiniggi*

(g) Pen, brown ink, with brown and gray wash, over black chalk
Inscribed, *Altro pensiero per li medesimi*

The two designs on one sheet of paper that was folded and then bound were for a villa that was never executed (see I. Belli Barsali, *La Villa a Lucca dal XV al XIX secolo*, Rome, 1964, pp. 167–169; in the section on villas near Viareggio, Belli Barsali did not connect any with Juvarra and the Guinigi family). Juvarra designed a number of villas and fountains for distinguished Lucchese families, many of which, like ours, remained unbuilt. His first recorded work in Lucca began in 1706 when he was asked, probably through the offices of his friend and patron, Coriolano Orsucci (see 36h), to complete the Palazzo Pubblico. In 1706 he also designed the façade for the church of SS. Trinità and a hospital, probably for SS. Trinità: projects unknown until our album was discovered (pp. 223, 224, 226). His association with the city continued for at least twenty years. Our drawings may be dated between 1706 and 1714, as the villa drawings for Cesare Benvegna and Cesare Benassai in the Biblioteca Nazionale, Turin, are dated 1714 (Riserva 59-4, leaves 12 and 65; Rovere, Viale, Brinckmann, pls. 148, 149; Messina, 1966, figs. 44, 46). Since the dated drawings in our album range from 1704 to 1708 and many others may be connected with early drawings, like those dated 1706 in the former Tournon album, I believe 36f and 36g should be dated closer to 1704 than to 1714.

The ground plan of 36f shows a central *salone* with two sets of diagonal projecting wings and with outbuildings encircling the building core. It recalls the drawing in the Museo Civico, Turin, the first idea for Juvarra's royal hunting lodge at Stupinigi designed for Vittorio Amadeo II between 1729 and 1733 (Vol. I, leaf 40, no. 56; see Pommer, *Eighteenth-Century Architecture in Piedmont*, pp. 61–78, 188, 189, fig. 78). The octagonal central *salone* of our drawing is, in the Stupinigi plans, either rectangular with semicircular ends (ibid., fig. 78, upper design) or oval (ibid., fig. 78, lower design). The elevations also resemble those he drew for Stupinigi (Museo Civico, Turin, Vol. I, leaf 7, no. 15; ibid., fig. 79) but the wings on our drawing are pulled in and shorter, and the stairway is different. The galleries of Stupinigi's courtyard are part of the building core, extending from it to form a great forecourt, while in our drawing they are separate, encircling the villa from behind.

The type of plan of our drawing was one Juvarra reworked a number of times. A basic axial plan underlay his design for the Concorso Clementino of 1705 (Rovere, Viale, Brinckmann, pls. 144, 145). In it, however, the courtyard was octagonal with only three radiating wings. The palazzo designed for the landgrave of Hesse-Cassel was an enormous complex, but essentially consisted of an octagonal central *salone* with four radiating wings combined with large rooms of various shapes between the wings (Biblioteca Nazionale, Turin, Riserva 59–4, leaf 83, no. 1; ibid., pp. 49, 50, dated about 1707, pl. 146). Brinckmann published two further drawings of this type, one as a "prelude" to Stupinigi (Riserva 59–4, leaf 51, no. 2; ibid., pl. 166) and another he thought to be connected to Stupinigi, a connection rejected by Pommer (Museo Civico, Turin, Vol. I, leaf 55, no. 81; ibid., pl. 167; Pommer, *Eighteenth-Century Architecture in Piedmont,* p. 218). Like our drawing, each has an octagonal *salone* with rooms radiating from it.

On both 36f and g, there are ziggurat, or stepped, cupolas. This is yet another theme which Juvarra used for many years. An etching by Giuseppe Vasi dated 1739, after Juvarra's design for a mausoleum for a French king, employs this ziggurat cupola (John Harris, "LeGeay, Piranesi and International Neo-Classicism in Rome, 1740–1750," *Essays Presented to Rudolf Wittkower on his Sixty-fifth Birthday,* I, London, 1967, p. 193, pl. XX, fig. 17). The drawing for this etching is in the Kunstbibliothek, Berlin, kindly pointed out to me by Sabine Jacob, who also indicated that several plates from Jacques Androuet Ducerceau's *Quoniam Apud Veteres Alio Structurae Genere Templa . . .* (Orleans, 1550) were among Juvarra's sources for the motif. The buttressing of the cupolas on the two end pavilions in the mausoleum design is similar to that on the central cupola of 36f.

36h Designs for clocks

(PAGE 187)

Pen, brown ink, over black chalk
Inscribed in brown ink, *Orologgio di tavolino/ per/ il Sig. Coriolano/ Orsucci*

These two sketches are the only metalwork designs in the album. Juvarra designed silver in Messina before leaving for Rome (see M. Accascina, "La Formazione Artistica di Filippo Juvarra," *Bollettino d'Arte* XLII, 1957, pp. 50–57; M. Accascina, *Profilo dell' Architettura a Messina,* pp. 85–89). Accascina connected with Juvarra several pieces of ecclesiastical work done in Messina prior to his departure: a silver frame, a monstrance, a chalice, and candelabra. They are all densely covered with small, ornate

decoration that contrasts with the less elaborate decoration of the architectonic forms of the clocks. Other metalwork designs by Juvarra are represented by drawings for chandeliers and centerpieces with candelabra in the Museo Civico and the Biblioteca Nazionale, Turin (see Rovere, Viale, Brinckmann, pls. 138–143; Messina, 1966, fig. 64).

The inscription on this sheet identifies the design as a small table clock for Signore Coriolano Orsucci. The anonymous eighteenth-century biography of Juvarra published by Rossi related that Juvarra returned to Messina when his father died in 1705. He returned to Rome in late 1705 or early 1706 with the Lucchese nobleman Coriolano Orsucci (Messina, 1966, pp. 24, 45). Orsucci became his friend and patron, and they remained close until Orsucci's death in 1717. Our sheet is datable from 1706 to Juvarra's departure from Rome in 1714.

Juvarra's clock designs are in the somewhat earlier tradition of French Louis XIV clocks. The composition of the clock at the bottom of the sheet, consisting of several columns or pilasters supporting a curved entablature, grows out of a tradition of French clocks that began about 1660. An example of this style is a pendulum clock by Baltazar Martinot of about 1675 (Clare Vincent, "Magnificent Timekeepers: an Exhibition of Northern European Clocks in New York Collections," *The Metropolitan Museum of Art Bulletin* XXX, 1971–72, p. 155, fig. 1). The Martinot clock lacks the curved entablature, which was a common motif of French clocks of a slightly later date (see Tardy, *La Pendule française,* 3rd ed., I, Paris, 1967, pls. 98–103). Tardy did not illustrate any French clocks that exhibit Juvarra's device of a curved entablature supported by columns, but a French tradition does exist for the idea. Daniel Marot's engravings of clocks in his *Oeuvre: Second Livre d'Orlogeries,* Amsterdam, 1712, reflect this combination of motifs (Klaus Maurice, *Die französische Pendule des 18. Jahrhunderts,* Berlin, 1967, pl. 36, fig. 52i). Although published in 1712, Marot's designs depend on the style current about 1690–1700. Juvarra's solution, seen in this sketch in which he paired the columns framing the clock face, is more architectural than Marot's. Juvarra experimented with two different heights for the dial, as indicated by the two circles on the clock. The sketchy lines atop the entablature indicate small, delicate finials. It is difficult to read the design surmounting the clock.

The clock represented in the upper sketch, with its pulled-in waist, also reflects French clocks of a slightly earlier period. One such, in the Metropolitan Museum, by André Charles Boulle with a movement by Jacques Thuret, is dated about 1690–95 (acc. no. 58.53; see James Parker, "A Royal French Clock," *The Metropolitan Museum of Art Bulletin* XVIII, 1959–60, pp. 193–201). The curve of the base of Juvarra's design is not one long sweep as in the Metropolitan's Boulle clock, but is instead divided into two connecting curves, somewhat similar to a design engraved by Marot (K. Maurice, *Die französische Pendule,* pl. 34, fig. 52d). The raised upper section capped by an elliptical curve is similar to a design after Thuret (Tardy, *La Pendule française,* I, p. 108, at lower left).

Italian clocks of this period have not been studied extensively and none reproduced by Tardy come as close to Juvarra's designs as do those engraved by Marot (*La Pendule française,* III, pp. 413–419). The engravings of clock designs by Giovanni Giardini in his *Disegni Diversi,* Rome, 1714 (pls. 70, 73, 81, and one unnumbered; see K. Maurice, *Die französische Pendule,* pl. 41) are similar to Juvarra's clocks in the suggestion of curling, foliated decoration. Giardini, however, used this decoration much more extensively; he also employed a raised upper section similar to that in this drawing.

A figure of Saturn stands on the base of the clock, and the clock itself is surmounted by putti holding an hour-glass and scythe, symbolizing Time the destroyer, who cuts life short.

It is impossible to say whether the fact that Juvarra's designs are close to the 1712 Marot engravings suggests that Juvarra's postdate Marot's and are dependent on them, or rather that they both reflect the same tradition.

36i and j Designs for coats of arms

(PAGES 167, 125)

(i) Pen, brown ink, over black chalk. Watermark: six-pointed star within a circle surmounted by a cross with an *F* below, near Heawood 3874

(j) Pen, brown ink, with brown and gray wash, over black chalk
Inscribed in brown ink, *dell' Autore*

The album contains twelve drawings of coats of arms destined for Juvarra's etchings in the book first published in 1711 by Antonio de' Rossi in Rome, *Raccolta di varie targhe di Roma fatte da professori primarj, disegnate, ed intagliate da Filippo Juvarra, architetto, e dedicate all'eminentissimo, e reverendissimo principe Pietro, card. Ottoboni, vice-cancelliere di S. Chiesa.* The book is dedicated to Juvarra's patron Cardinal Ottoboni, for whose theater in the Palazzo Cancelleria Juvarra designed stage sets, his principal occupation at that time. The 1711 edition of the *Raccolta di varie targhe* is rare and is not noted in the Juvarra literature (copies are in Avery Library and the Biblioteca Casanatense, Rome). A copy of the edition of 1715, also unrecorded in the Juvarra literature, published by Giovanni Maria Salvioni and dedicated to Alessandro (later Cardinal) Albani, is in the Metropolitan Museum. Both the 1711 and 1715 editions contain fifty numbered plates of *targhe,* or coats of arms, and an unnumbered one demonstrating the principles of *targhe* design. The 1722 edition was published by Salvioni (as were all the succeed-

ing editions), but dedicated to Giuseppe Lotario Conti, duke of Poli and brother of the new pope, Innocent XIII. In addition to the fifty plates by Juvarra, the 1722 edition contains two etched by Filippo Vasconi, one of which is after a design of Juvarra, the other after one by G. B. Puccetti (Rovere, Viale, Brinckmann, p. 164; Messina, 1966, p. 119). There are in some of these later editions four additional unsigned plates. Succeeding editions were published in 1727, 1732, and then in 1881 by the Roman Calcografia, which still possesses all the plates, with the exception of the title page.

Juvarra projected the book as early as 1706 when he designed a frontispiece inscribed *Targe di Roma raccolte da me D. Filippo Yuvarra 1706* (Museo Civico, Turin, Vol. II, leaf 23, no. 12; Rovere, Viale, Brinckmann, p. 48; Messina, 1966, p. 46). Lightly sketched above the cartouche containing the inscription is a cardinal's hat, but as Juvarra's patronage by Cardinal Ottoboni probably began only in 1708 it may not allude to Ottoboni (Messina, 1966, p. 48). The frontispiece is decorated with symbols of the arts.

The original fifty plates of the *Raccolta di varie targhe* reproduce coats of arms adorning Roman buildings and monuments designed by Michelangelo, Bernini, Borromini, Pietro da Cortona, Carlo and Francesco Fontana, Alessandro Algardi, and others, including one designed by Juvarra himself.

In addition to the preliminary drawings for the *Raccolta di varie targhe* in our volume, there are twenty-three in Volumes I and II in the Museo Civico and four in Riserva 59–4 in the Biblioteca Nazionale. All these albums contain, in addition, a number of sketches for *targhe* that were not etched. The preliminary drawing for the vignette with the arms of Cardinal Ottoboni that embellished the title page of the 1711 edition appears on leaf 57 of Riserva 59–4. On leaf 29 of that volume are the preliminary sketches for the unnumbered plate on which Juvarra demonstrated how to design *targhe.*

Juvarra took into consideration the problem of reversal in printmaking, and most of the etchings are in the same direction as our drawings and the coats of arms they reproduce. 36i was etched as plate 15 and shows the Pamphili arms on the north side of Bernini's Four Rivers Fountain in Piazza Navona. A drawing in the Museo Civico (Vol. II, leaf 29, no. 55) is for the same plate but reversed. It has been incised by tracing with a stylus for transfer, as have all the other Museo Civico drawings. It alone differs from the rest of the group of Museo Civico drawings which have rectangular black-chalk borders, roughly conforming in size and shape to the copper plates. The Museo Civico drawings are clearly Juvarra's preparatory drawings for the etchings, which he made from the drawings in both our album and the Biblioteca Nazionale's Riserva 59–4. These are earlier studies, probably made from the *targhe* themselves.

Our album contains studies for plates 8, 13, 15, 17, 18, 25, 26, 27, 30, 31, 34 and 40 in the *Raccolta di varie targhe* (pages 165, 149, 167, 111, 113, 157, 101, 147, 117, 143, 60, and 137). The final plate Juvarra etched was his own invention, which he described as being in the port of Messina. His version of the arms of Messina shows a cross within the cartouche with crossed trident and oar and dolphins at either side. The sea imagery of the Messina arms of shell, dolphins, and trident is repeated on 36j, inscribed *dell'autore,* which is the way he described himself when identifying plate 50 in the book. The blank shell cartouche with dolphins at either side, their tails entwined around a trident that surmounts the cartouche, must allude to Juvarra's native city. There are a number of other variant studies of the arms of Messina. The closest to that etched is in the Museo Civico (Vol. II, leaf 88, no. 178). It has a rectangular border similar to the other preparatory drawings. Two further studies close to that etched are also in the Museo Civico (Vol. II, leaves 22, no. 40, and 86, no. 174). Whether they are Juvarra's own inventions or studies after other arms in the city is not clear. They look to me, however, like Juvarra's own reworking of the Messina arms. One other such, very close to our sketch, is in the Museo Civico (Vol. IV, leaf 42, no. 46). Juvarra's pupil Ignazio Agliaudi, baron di Tavigliano, copied a number of the *targhe* in a volume in the Biblioteca Nazionale (Riserva 59–10).

36k and l Designs for the Cappella Antamoro in S. Girolamo della Carità, Rome

(PAGES 235, 249)

(k) Pen, brown ink, with brown and gray wash, over black chalk
Inscribed in brown ink, *Primo pensiero per la Capella di S. Filippo a S. Girolamo/ del Sig. Avocato Antemoro, messa in opera l'año 1708*

(l) Pen, brown ink, with brown and gray wash, over black chalk. Watermark: six-pointed star within a circle surmounted by a cross with an *F* below, near Heawood 3874
Inscribed in brown ink, *Secondo pensiero / della Capella di S. Fipo / in S. Girolamo*

In 1703 Tommaso Antamoro reserved space to the left of the high altar in the church of S. Girolamo della Carità for his chapel (see S. de Vito Battaglia, "Un' opera romana di Filippo Juvarra," *Bollettino d'Arte* XXX, 1936–37, pp. 485–498; and R. Preimesberger, "Entwürfe Pierre Legros' für Filippo Juvarras Cappella Antamoro," *Römische Historische Mitteilungen* X, 1966–67, pp. 200–215). As the inscription on 36k indicates, Juvarra had received the commission and made his design by 1708, at which time the chapel was begun. It was finished and dedicated in 1710 and is the only architecture executed by Juvarra in Rome. Until our album appeared, the only known Juvarra drawings for the chapel were those in the Biblioteca Nazionale, Turin (Riserva 59–4). Most of these are detail studies for the doors, capitals, putti over the entrance, and candelabra; only one is a view of the entire chapel (leaf 127, no. 1), but it is very sketchy.

Dedicated to S. Filippo Neri, whose statue by Pierre Legros is on the altar, the chapel is very small, measuring approximately seventeen by ten and a half feet (measurements given by de Vito Battaglia, "Un' opera romana," p. 485). The chapel's effect is extremely rich, with its primarily red-brown and green polychrome marbles and its bronze doors with gilt ornaments.

A ground plan on p. 247 in our album has measurements in *palmi* and gives the basic rectangular shape of the chapel, which was rounded at the altar end. It contains a detailed study of an altar plan with indications for two columns, which does not conform to either 36k, Juvarra's first idea for the chapel, or 36l, his second. However, above this plan is another, showing a column set against a rounded wall as well as a circle surrounded by putti's heads that is similar to the oculus that crowns the vault of the Cappella Antamoro, indicating that part of this drawing, at least, is probably connected with the chapel. The *palmi* measurements approximate those of the chapel.

36k and l show that from the beginning, Juvarra planned to set the statue of S. Filippo against an oval translucent glory that would rise midway into the vaulting. Our two drawings show that he eliminated the lunettes above the architrave seen in 36k and added freestanding columns at the corners on either side of the oval glory seen in 36l. Both changes help focus on the figure of the ascending saint. Although 36l does not show the oval behind the figure of S. Filippo, it was probably not eliminated by Juvarra from this scheme, but as he had already worked out the idea as central to the architectural program, he perhaps omitted it out of haste. The Turin sketch records certain details further advanced than in either of our drawings, the most prominent of which are the volutes that terminate the oval at the altar, in place of the simple, closed oval seen in 36k. There are no indications in our drawings of the volutes terminating the vaulting in the chapel.

Preimesberger traced the architectural antecedents of the Cappella Antamoro, but without knowing of the existence of our two drawings. They indicate a much stronger dependence on Bernini's forms than on Fontana's. The high altars in S. Andrea al Quirinale and in S. Tommaso di Villanova at Castel Gandolfo, both of which Juvarra drew on leaves of this album, the Cappella Fonseca in S. Lorenzo in Lucina, the Cappella Silva in S. Isidoro, as well as the *Cathedra* in St. Peter's, are all much closer antecedents to the first designs for the chapel revealed in our drawings. The visual as well as spatial unity achieved by Juvarra in the chapel was implicit in 36k, and the subsequent changes were essentially refinements.

GIOVANNI BATTISTA MADERNA
(Verona 1758–1803 Stockholm)

37 Design for decoration of a drawing room

Pen, brown ink, with brown and colored wash.
11½ x 19 in. (291 x 482 mm)
Inscribed in brown ink at bottom below drawn border,
Drawing Room; signed in brown ink at lower right within
border, *Gio Batt Maderna F.*

BIBLIOGRAPHY: J. Harris, *A Catalogue of British
Drawings for Architecture, Decoration, Sculpture, . . . in
American Collections,* Upper Saddle River, N.J. [1971], p.
134, pl. 95
The Elisha Whittelsey Collection, The Elisha Whittelsey
Fund, 49.56.16

Typical of many itinerant Italian artists in the eighteenth
century who painted decoration throughout Europe, Maderna (his name was sometimes spelled Maderni) worked
in Paris, London, St. Petersburg, and Stockholm, after
studying in Florence and Rome. The inscription indicates
our drawing was made to decorate an English drawing
room. Little is known of Maderna's work in England, and
the house for which the drawing was made has not been
identified.

The area at the right of the drawing, darkened by a layer
of brown wash drawn diagonally across the design, indicates that what appears to be one wall is, in fact, two adjacent walls. The wall at left contains the fenestration and
the one at right, a doorway. Alternate treatments of the
decoration are illustrated in the two sections.

CARLO MARCHIONNI
(Rome 1702–1786 Rome)

38 Designs for festival decorations on the bases of piers

Pen, brown ink, with gray wash, over black chalk.
13½ x 15⅜ in. (343 x 391 mm)
The Elisha Whittelsey Collection, The Elisha Whittelsey
Fund, 68.683.1

Carlo Marchionni was a prolific architectural draughtsman,
as the large collections of drawings in the Cooper-Hewitt
Museum, University of Würzburg, Museo di Roma, and
other collections attest. He studied with the architect
Filippo Barigioni, who had worked in Carlo Fontana's
studio (see No. 29). Marchionni's talent was recognized
in 1728 when he won the Accademia di S. Luca's first prize
for architecture in the Concorso Clementino. His great
works are the Villa Albani (about 1746–63), the most renowned Roman eighteenth-century villa, and the Sacristy
of St. Peter's (1776–84). In 1773 he became architect of
St. Peter's after the death of Luigi Vanvitelli (see Nos.
60–75), whose assistant in that capacity Marchionni had

been for nearly twenty years. He was also a sometime
sculptor, working with Pietro Bracci. Like many eighteenth-century architects, he often carried out temporary
decorations for secular and religious ceremonies: many
drawings exist for catafalques and other funeral decorations (see R. Berliner, "Zeichnungen von Carlo und
Filippo Marchionni," *Münchner Jahrbuch der bildenden
Kunst* IX/X, 1958/59, pp. 330–343). Notable among these
are one for Augustus III, king of Poland and elector of
Saxony, and one for Carlo Emanuele III of Savoy.

The partial decorations on four piers, in this drawing
quite tightly spaced to economize on paper, give no clue in
themselves to the particular use they so lavishly served, and
would never have been identified were it not for the existence of a larger drawing in the Cini Foundation depicting
a portion of the church's interior (inv. no. 36.178). Traditionally attributed on the basis of an inscription on the
verso to the Bolognese Vittorio Bigari, and published as
such (C. Johnston, *I Disegni dei Maestri: il Seicento e il
Settecento a Bologna,* Milan, 1970, p. 77, fig. 28, p. 92),
the drawing is nevertheless entirely consistent with Marchionni's draughtsmanship. The Metropolitan sheet shows
only the ornamentation of the bases of the piers, the
wreaths on the bases recalling the Borrominian motif between the windows of the nave of the Lateran, while the
Cini drawing represents the longitudinal section of a
church in which two bays are delineated, and half of another sketched in. In the Cini drawing, the middle pier,
with its engaged half columns, has the same decorations of
cartouche with putti enveloped in draperies as does the
middle pier of our drawing. The lone figure standing with
arm outstretched in our drawing joins a large crowd of
prelates and other noblemen in the Cini sheet. In the latter
drawing an orchestra is represented on a raised and decorated platform in the bay at the left. Suspended from the
arches are hangings containing cartouches with scenes of
a saint. At the left is depicted an angel appearing to a
female saint kneeling before an altar; in the center, as
Johnston has noted, the female saint receives the halo from
the Virgin. Johnston astutely identified the symbol of the
Dominican order above the right arch. Also notable in the
Cini drawing is the pointed Gothic vaulting of the church.

The great Dominican church in Rome is S. Maria sopra
Minerva, one of the few medieval churches still extant
there. In 1746, Marchionni was commissioned, probably
through the good offices of Prince Alessandro Ruspoli, to
decorate S. Maria sopra Minerva for the celebration of the
canonization of the Dominican saint, Caterina de' Ricci
(Berliner, "Zeichnungen von . . . Marchionni," p. 283).
Berliner cited a contemporary account of the *festa,* describing the magnificent decorations that especially pleased
Pope Benedict XIV who, as Cardinal Lambertini, had pro-
moted Caterina de' Ricci's beatification and, as pope, her

canonization. Saint Caterina de' Ricci, of a noble Florentine family and a devotee of Savanarola's writings, was noted for her many visions. The two painted scenes hanging from the arches in the Cini drawing represent two of these. Marchionni had already worked in S. Maria sopra Minerva, erecting there in 1738–39 the monument to Pope Benedict XIII, with sculpture by Pietro Bracci.

39 Designs for visiting cards

Pen, brown ink, with gray wash. 6⅜ x 9⅛ in. (162 x 232 mm). Inlaid into paper with decorated French mount, from a volume in an early nineteenth-century calf binding
Inscribed on mount in pencil, *8 pieces dans ce volume*

PROVENANCE: H. Destailleur, Paris (see Lugt 740)
The Elisha Whittelsey Collection, The Elisha Whittelsey Fund, 48.148(73)

This sheet was identified by Rudolf Berliner, who connected these designs for visiting cards—*cartes de visites*—with others by Marchionni in the University of Würzburg and the Cooper-Hewitt Museum (R. Berliner, "Zeichnungen von...Marchionni," pp. 360–368). Berliner noted Marchionni's effort to monumentalize, literally, this rather minor genre: in many of his *cartes de visites,* Marchionni used monuments as the basis of his design. The design at the upper left illustrates this, as does to a lesser extent that at the lower right. The classical temple and the sphinx in the upper left drawing suggest symbols of Rome, while those in the design at the upper right are specifically Bolognese: *LIBERTAS* is Bologna's motto, appearing on her coat of arms, and the two leaning towers sketched in at the left of the design are such distinctive features of that city's skyline that they, too, have come to symbolize the city. There are, however, no clues to identify the person for whom these cards were designed.

LEONARDO MARINI
(Turin, active 1760–98)

40 Design for a ceiling decoration of a reception room at the royal palace at Moncalieri, 1778

Black chalk. 13¾ x 19¹⁵⁄₁₆ in. (349 x 506 mm)
Inscribed in pen and brown ink at bottom, *Giampiero Pozzo;* at right, *Disegno aprovato per il contorno della Camera di Parata di S.A.R. il Sig. Principe di Piemonte a Moncaglieri/ il 2 Aprile 1778/ Bertolino avio non si vari*
PROVENANCE: Leon Dalva, New York, Piedmontese scrapbook
Gift of Leon Dalva, 65.654.13

The identification of Marini as the author of this drawing is due to Mercedes Viale Ferrero who pointed out to me that a manuscript volume by Marini in the Biblioteca Reale, Turin (Ms varia 218) contained further drawings for his decorations at Moncalieri, the royal palace of the house of Savoy near Turin. The Metropolitan has several other drawings by Marini, some with inscriptions connecting them to Moncalieri, and others which can be attributed to that project.

Marini is known primarily for his work for the Teatro Regio in Turin (see M. Viale Ferrero, *La Scenografia del '700,* pp. 68–76; *Mostra del Barocco Piemontese,* I, Turin, 1963, the section "Scenografia" by Mercedes Viale Ferrero, pp. 41–44). He became the *Disegnatore ordinario delle camere* in 1782, after having become a professor in the Royal Academy of Painting at its inception in 1778. He was a talented designer of interiors and a draughtsman who revelled in a luxurious use of colored washes.

This is Marini's approved working drawing that was given to the actual painter of the rooms, Giovanni Pietro Pozzo—hence Pozzo's name on the drawing—to work from when decorating the palace. Pozzo, born in Milan in 1713 and died in Turin in 1798 (see Baudi di Vesme, *Schede Vesme: L'Arte in Piemonte...,* III, Turin, 1968, pp. 862–863), was paid on 17 May and on 9 September 1778 for his work at Moncalieri (ibid., p. 863). Marini was paid on 4 December 1778 for his designs (Turin, Archivio di Stato, Real Casa for the year 1778). Work began on Moncalieri in 1774 and continued into the mid-1780s. Parts of the castle, which is now a military headquarters, were redecorated in the nineteenth century.

41 Design for one-quarter of a ceiling decoration

Pen, brown ink, with wash, over graphite. 8½ x 10 in. (216 x 254 mm)
PROVENANCE: Leon Dalva, New York, Piedmontese scrapbook
Gift of Leon Dalva, 65.654.115

This drawing is attributed to Marini on the basis of comparison with the drawings in the Biblioteca Reale, Turin (Ms varia 218). The use of sphinxes on either side of an urn is a repeated motif in Marini's work, as are the wreaths and the barely visible ram's head in the corner. There are many such quick sketches in pen and ink among the Biblioteca Reale drawings, several of which are for Moncalieri.

42 Design for a palace interior decoration

Pen, gray ink, with gray and colored wash. 14¼ x 10½ in.
(362 x 267 mm)
Signed in brown ink at lower right, *L. Marini fe*
PROVENANCE: Leon Dalva, New York, Piedmontese
scrapbook
Gift of Leon Dalva, 65.654.36

This sumptuous interior elevation may be one of Marini's
finished designs for a reception room in the royal palace at
Moncalieri. Very similar decorations for Moncalieri are in
the collection of the Biblioteca Reale (Ms varia 218).

43 Design for decoration of the interior of the gallery of a palace

Pen, brown and gray ink, with gray, beige, and colored wash.
11⅝ x 17¼ in. (295 x 438 mm)
Inscribed in brown ink at upper left, *Galeria di Somariva di
Perno Casa S. Tomaso*; in black chalk within the drawing,
statua, trofei, arabeschi, basso rilievo, [unintelligible]
arabeschi
PROVENANCE: Leon Dalva, New York, Piedmontese
scrapbook
Gift of Leon Dalva, 65.654.15

The inscription on this beautiful drawing showing the elevation of the wall, cove of the ceiling, and the end wall, was
at first extremely puzzling. *Galeria di Somariva* referred,
many scholars who had seen the drawing felt, to Count
Giovanni Battista Sommariva (1760–1826), a self-made
man who came to political power during the tumultuous
days of Napoleonic rule in Italy. Sommariva spent his huge
fortune collecting the greatest contemporary French painters' works, which were installed in his sumptuous villa on
Lake Como, near Tremezzo (see Francis Haskell, *An Italian Patron of French Neo-Classic Art: The Zaharoff Lec-
ture for 1972*, Oxford, 1972, p. 10). The *galleria* in the
inscription has been presumed to refer to that in the Villa
Carlotta, as it had come to be known after it was sold by
Sommariva's heirs.

However, the interior of the gallery at Villa Carlotta,
which remains unchanged, does not resemble the decoration in this drawing at all (see A. Ottino Della Chiesa,
Villa Carlotta, Tremezzo-Cadenabbia, n.d.). The rest of the
inscription makes little sense. No Casa S. Tomaso is mentioned in guidebooks in the vicinity of Villa Carlotta, nor
is a town called Perno. Furthermore, Perno is not a town
found in Lombard guidebooks. However, the small town
of Sommariva Perno does exist in Southern Piedmont near
Bra. It is so small that it is described only briefly in guides,
in which there is neither mention of a church of S. Tomaso
nor of a magnificent house standing near it.

Thus a drawing which at first appeared to be connected
with a great patron of the arts and to be for his renowned

Lombard villa, is instead for an anonymous house in a
small Piedmontese town. However, if this drawing was
executed, that small town must have contained a house
with a gallery of extraordinary beauty.

This drawing is dated about 1785–95 because of the
close dependence on Albertolli's style which was at that
time being disseminated through the publication of his designs (see No. 1). Marini's works of the 1770s (such as
No. 40) are fully in the tradition of North Italian late
baroque decoration, but it would have been only natural
for Marini to have responded to Albertolli's style. Some
small pen and ink sketches in a volume in the Biblioteca
Reale, Turin (Ms varia 218) demonstrate his response:
one of the drawings, a design for a ceiling at Moncalieri
dated 1783, is compartmentalized and employs classical
elements in a sober fashion very much in the Albertollian
canon. However, the Piedmontese Marini, as is shown in
our drawing, filters Albertolli's Roman sobriety through
a sensibility more akin to the French, and one which is at
once gaier and more elegant.

FLAMINIO INNOCENZO MINOZZI
(Bologna 1735–1817 Bologna)

44a and b Designs for altars

(a) Pen, brown ink, with brown, gray, yellow, and rose wash.
13½ x 5¾ in. (343 x 146 mm). Horizontal crease at center
with small tears along it. Laid down with small border
showing with a partial Gothic A stamped in purple ink at
lower right

(b) Pen, brown ink, with brown, gray, rose, and green wash,
over traces of black chalk. 13⁷⁄₁₆ x 8¹⁄₁₆ in. (341 x 205 mm).
Laid down with small border showing with a Gothic A
stamped in purple ink at lower left. Some tears and holes
PROVENANCE: Janos Scholz, New York
The Elisha Whittelsey Collection, The Elisha Whittelsey
Fund, 52.570.72, 74

Minozzi, Carlo Bianconi (Nos. 5–8), and Mauro Tesi (Nos.
57–58) are the most notable Bolognese draughtsmen in
this exhibition, apart from the Bibiena family. Flaminio's
father, Bernardo Minozzi (1699–1769), painted landscapes and architecture and was an etcher as well. Several
of his landscape drawings are in the Louvre. Flaminio
studied figure painting, but according to Luigi Crespi
(*Felsina Pittrice. . .*, III, Rome, 1769, p. 196), as a young
man he showed a decided inclination towards architecture.
For several years he studied with Carlo Bibiena. At the age
of fifteen, in his first attempt, he won first prize for architecture at the Accademia Clementina. Crespi related that
for the next seven years he continued to win top prize. Two
of his prize-winning drawings for the competitions of
1755 and 1756 are in the Accademia di Belle Arti, Bologna: a design for a town gate, and one for a large palace,

showing transverse and longitudinal sections. Both designs are accomplished and show a firm grounding in late baroque architecture. His essays in pure ornament may be seen in Pio Panfili's book of etchings, *Frammenti di ornati per li giovani principianti nel Disegno* (Bologna, 1783), for which Flaminio designed the title page and a chalice and candelabra on plate 14, on which Mauro Tesi also contributed a design.

These two studies for altars, formerly anonymous and here attributed to Minozzi, must have been made fairly early in his career, probably about 1765–75. The curling, foliated cartouche surmounting the altar in both 44a and b and the application of rococo forms to a nascent neoclassic structure link these sheets to a Minozzi drawing of an illusionistic dome, signed and dated 1772, in the University of Michigan Museum (R. Wunder, *Architectural and Ornament Drawings of the 16th to the early 19th Centuries in the Collection of The University of Michigan Museum of Art*, Ann Arbor, 1965, no. 63, repr.). Our drawings exhibit the same fluid and brilliant draughtsmanship as the Michigan drawing. Minozzi's style became increasingly neoclassic, and in his last years, very hard and dry, as seen in some drawings in the Cooper-Hewitt Museum, dated the first decade of the nineteenth century.

It is possible that both these designs were for illusionistic painted decoration. The altar frame of No. 44a could have been painted on the chapel wall with a panel painting hung in the space left blank and a simple tabular altar set in front. Mark Weil, who is preparing a study on the *Quarant'Ore*, recently pointed out to me that the glory surmounting the altar in 44b suggests that the drawing may be for a *Quarant'Ore* celebration (see No. 79).

FLAMINIO INNOCENZO MINOZZI
(attributed to)

45 Design for a ceiling

Pen, brown ink, with brown, gray, rose, and blue wash, over traces of black chalk. 9¹⁵⁄₁₆ x 11¹³⁄₁₆ in. (237 x 300 mm). Inlaid into modern mount. Watermark: escutcheon with fleur-de-lys, bottom cut off, near Heawood 1743
Inscribed in faint black chalk on column base at right of central medallion, *F* (?) . . . ; verso, in brown ink, erased, at lower left, *Cop* (?) . . . ; on a line below, *F. M . . . ssi* (?)

EXHIBITIONS: Portsmouth, 1969, no. 39, repr.
Harris Brisbane Dick Fund and Joseph Pulitzer Bequest, 1971.513.55

The attribution of this drawing to Minozzi presents some difficulties. The ceiling conforms to Minozzi's decorative style; the architectural rendering and perspective, as suggested by the faint black chalk lines in the central panel, are done with care and skill. However, it is not the finest example of his work; in particular, the figures are rendered

with a slight awkwardness one does not expect of Minozzi, whose figural draughtsmanship, however, is not known. The style is very close to Minozzi's, and the draughtsmanship is masterful.

A coarse version of the right half of this drawing that depicts only one-quarter of the ceiling is in the Cini Foundation, and is traditionally attributed to Minozzi (inv. no. 33.410). The Cini sheet, dated 1783 (with an illegible inscription), is surely too crude to be by Minozzi, but is of especial interest as it suggests a date for Minozzi's project.

The problem in identifying Bolognese drawings is the prevalence of copies. Bolognese artists taught themselves by copying earlier masters, and often an innocent identification by the copyist causes confusion in present-day efforts to identify the author of the sheet. In this light, it is to be lamented that the inscription on the verso is largely erased.

GIOVANNI BATTISTA NATALI III
(Pontremoli 1698–1765 Naples)

46 Design for a portable screen

Brush and gray ink. 10½ x 9⁷⁄₁₆ in. (267 x 240 mm). Folded into seven vertical sections
Inscribed in brown ink vertically at left, *Disego di Paravto di Natali 1741*
The Elisha Whittelsey Collection, The Elisha Whittelsey Fund, 49.63.278

The youngest and last prominent member of a Cremonese family of artists, Giovanni Battista Natali III was primarily a painter of architectural decoration and, according to Mariette, a designer for the theater, a contention borne out by some of his extant drawings. Natali was a pupil of the itinerant Florentine painter Sebastiano Galeotti, for whose ceiling of 1736, representing the Marriage of Cupid and Psyche in the *Salotto* of Palazzo Spinola, Genoa, he provided the painted architectural ornament. Natali is recorded the following year in Naples, where he collaborated with Santolo Cirillo on a ceiling decoration in S. Paolo Maggiore. Returning to his native town of Pontremoli (north of La Spezia just within the border of Tuscany), he built and decorated the portico of the church of S. Francesco in 1747. He returned to Naples in the 1750s where, as painter to the court, he produced his best-known work. More of Natali's projects are becoming known as his drawings are discovered and studied. For example, the Cooper-Hewitt Museum has drawings for two different Neapolitan projects. He is not to be confused with his uncle Giuseppe Natali (1652–1722) who signed the first drawing in an album (which gives it the name the *Natali* album) in the drawings collection of the Royal Institute of British Architects.

37

The identification of this drawing by its inscription has been upheld by comparison with four similar drawings by Natali in the Cooper-Hewitt Museum for the Seggio di Porto in Naples (Elaine Evans Dee, *The Two Sicilies* [exhibition catalogue], Finch College Museum of Art, New York, 1970, nos. 42, 43, 45, 46). In Walter Vitzthum's review of the exhibition (*Burlington Magazine* CXII, 1970, p. 264), he published two further drawings for the same project that are in the Art Gallery of Ontario, Toronto. See his entry in *Drawings in the Collection of the Art Gallery of Ontario* [exhibition catalogue], Toronto, 1970, no. 20, repr.).

It is clear that the Metropolitan, Cooper-Hewitt, and Toronto sheets are by the same artist. The use of brush and gray wash, sometimes without any penwork, is characteristic of one of Natali's drawing styles. The same free and loose pen- and brushstrokes are evident in all the drawings, as are the intermingled repetitions of late baroque and rococo architectural details. Curved and intricate forms predominate: the central panel of the screen is surmounted not by a simple pediment, but by a broken, addossed segmental one enclosing a head crowned with a C-scroll (the latter is a favorite and often-repeated motif). The rococo flavor is enforced by the lively foliated forms which seem to grow up and down the second panel.

This drawing comes from a group of drawings including six others by Natali and the mirror frame by Giannotti (No. 34). Two of those Natali drawings (not exhibited) contain the arms of the distinguished Lucchese family, the Bernardini, and it is probable that this elaborate and beautiful screen was designed for their palazzo in Lucca. In a biography of Natali (R. Soprani and C. G. Ratti, *Delle Vite de' Pittori, Scultori, ed Architetti Genovesi*, II, Genoa, 1769, p. 370) it is stated that Natali was very active in Tuscany, especially in Lucca. This drawing and its companions in the group confirm this fact, which has generally been overlooked in the emphasis on his work for the Neapolitan court.

This drawing has been creased vertically seven times, coinciding with the divisions of the screen, done presumably to give the effect of the screen as it would stand partially folded.

47 Design for a canopy

Brush and gray ink. 5¾ x 8¼ in. (146 x 210 mm). Vertical and horizontal creases.
Inscribed in brown ink at upper right, *Sig. Natali*; at lower left, *sopracielo Impto*
Verso: Design for an armchair
Inscribed, *capezziera*
The Elisha Whittelsey Collection, The Elisha Whittelsey Fund, 49.63.276

The canopy and chair were probably designed for the Ber-

nardini family in Lucca, since the drawing was part of the same group as No. 46. It is also likely that all of this furniture—carved screen, canopy, and chair—was designed by Natali to be carved by Giannotti (No. 34), since Natali is known only for his painting and some architecture, while Giannotti was a woodcarver of note.

48 Design for a stage set: stairway and arcades leading to a *salone*

Pen, brown ink, with brown and gray wash. 5⅞ x 4 in. (149 x 102 mm)
Inscribed, recto, faintly in pencil at center bottom, 5; verso, in brown ink at top of sheet, *Cantava .3. Rotalo 9: Fighi Mondi/ neti* [unintelligible letter] *21: 6* [rest obscured by paper strip] / *Per tella fine Spago intalatura*

PROVENANCE: Edmond Fatio, Geneva (his mark lower right); Fatio sale, Geneva, Rauch, 3–4 June 1959, lot 12; New York, William Schab Gallery, *Catalogue No. 33* [1963], no. 137, repr.
Purchase, Gift of the Ian Woodner Family Foundation, 1974.605.2

When in the Fatio collection, this drawing and Nos. 49, 50a and b, and 51 were part of a group of eighteen designs by the same hand, bound together in a scrapbook with four other different ornament drawings. The Metropolitan recently acquired seventeen of the eighteen drawings (the other was sold at the benefit auction for the Cooper-Hewitt Museum, 19 March 1974, lot 108, repr.) that are clearly by Giovanni Battista Natali. In the exhibitions in Florence and Zurich of the Fatio collection, companion drawings by Natali were attributed to Ferdinando Bibiena (*Architektur und Dekorations-Zeichnungen der Barockzeit aus der Sammlung Edmond Fatio, Genf,* Zurich, Graphische Sammlung der Eidgenössische Technische Hochschule in Zürich, 1946, nos. 44–50; *I Disegni Scenografi della raccolta Fatio,* Florence, La Strozzina, nos. 49a–c, 52a–c, 72a–c, some repr.). To connect these drawings with a member of the greatest Italian family of stage designers underscores the brilliant draughtsmanship exhibited here. The nervous intensity of the pen- and brushwork, the vivacity in the use of the wash, the sure rendering of elaborate architectural spaces, the love of vaulted vistas stretching to infinity, must have made the attribution seem a probable one. However, the hand is certainly not that of Ferdinando or any other member of the Bibiena family.

Elaine Evans Dee and I jointly identified these drawings as Natali on the basis of similarities to the Natali drawings in the Cooper-Hewitt and Toronto collections. The deft use of pen and brush, the repetition of the motif of an oval cartouche supported on both sides by putti, crowning an arch, as well as the arch itself, which is characteristically formed by two long C-scrolls meeting at the crown, are features seen in most Natali drawings.

The group of seventeen drawings comprises a virtual catalogue of Natali's range. Some are extremely sketchy and schematic while others, such as this one, are rich, elaborate studies of complex architectural renderings. Natali responded freely to his architectural heritage: in certain of the drawings Natali paid homage to Juvarra (Natali worked in Piedmont, as well as Lucca), while in others his style suggests the reason for their previous attribution to the Bibienas. The present drawing is reminiscent of the magnificent and intricate entrances of the Neapolitan architect Ferdinando Sanfelice. There are further Neapolitan details in other of the drawings, as well as certain features recalling Natali's Neapolitan drawings at Cooper-Hewitt and Toronto. It is therefore likely that this group belongs to Natali's Neapolitan period.

A preliminary study for the present drawing was recently on the Milan art market where it was attributed to the French architect Charles Michel-Ange Challe (*Cinque Secoli di Architettura nel disegno . . .* [exhibition catalogue] [1972], Milan, Stanza del Borgo, no. 16, repr.). It is interesting to note that, according to the catalogue, the drawing came from an album of sketches by the Bibienas.

49 Design for a stage set: interior of a palazzo decorated with large mirrors and console tables

Pen, brown ink, with gray wash. 5⅛ x 4 in. (130 x 102 mm)

PROVENANCE: Edmond Fatio, Geneva (his mark lower right); Fatio sale, Geneva, Rauch, 3–4 June 1959, lot 12; New York, William Schab Gallery, *Catalogue No. 33* [1963], no. 137, repr.
Purchase, Gift of the Ian Woodner Family Foundation, 1974.605.3

The same rococo sensibility as the one that produced the furniture designs in Nos. 46 and 47 is at work here, to the extent that one could visualize those pieces installed in this beautiful room. However, the functions of the drawings are very different. In all probability this design is for a stage set, as are most of the other drawings in the group.

50a and b Designs for stage sets

(a) Anteroom with stairs leading to a gallery composed of a series of connected barrel vaults
Pen and brush, gray ink, with brown and gray wash.
6³⁄₁₆ x 4⁵⁄₁₆ in. (157 x 110 mm)

(b) Groin-vaulted stairway leading to a gallery with another stairway to a second story at left
Brush, gray ink, with gray wash. 6⅛ x 4⅜ in.
(156 x 111 mm). Laid down
Inscribed in brown ink at lower left, *I*
Verso: Sketches. Black chalk and gray ink

PROVENANCE: Edmond Fatio, Geneva (his mark lower right); Fatio sale, Geneva, Rauch, 3–4 June 1959, lot 12; New York, William Schab Gallery, *Catalogue No. 33* [1963], no. 137
Purchase, Gift of the Ian Woodner Family Foundation, 1974.605.1, 4

These two drawings establish that the Fatio drawings by Natali are mostly stage sets. The French collector P.-J. Mariette stated that Natali was a stage designer (P. de Chennevières and A. de Montaiglon, *Abecedario de Mariette . . .*, IV, Paris, 1857–58, p. 38). The beginnings of a ground plan are to be seen at the bottom of 50b and the letter *I* is probably a key for inscriptions on another drawing. Such initials to indicate position are often seen on stage designs (see, for example, Nos. 11, 12). Although it is most probable that 50a is also a design for a set, it could possibly be an elaborate perspective for a painted wall decoration such as the one Natali designed for the Seggio di Porto in Naples (see No. 46). The function of elaborate architectural perspectives is often difficult to determine since the same design could be used either on the stage or on the walls of a great palazzo.

Natali's different styles of draughtsmanship are demonstrated by these two sheets. The summary use of brush and only gray ink gives 50b a muddied appearance in contrast to the crisper, brighter effect of the penwork and the addition of brown ink in 50a. The latter, however, is treated in a sketchier, more summary manner than that of the more highly finished drawings, Nos. 48 and 49. The importance of the entire Fatio group of drawings will be to provide a frame of reference for future studies of the varying styles of draughtsmanship that Natali employed, enabling the identification of other of his as yet unrecognized drawings. Already it has been possible to identify several other Natali drawings on the basis of the Fatio group, including two in The Metropolitan Museum of Art (Nos. 52a and b) and two others, formerly attributed to the Bibienas: one at Princeton (acc. no. 53.106), and the other in the British Museum (no. 1939-3-11-23).

51 Ornament design with alternate suggestion

Brush, gray ink, gray wash. 4⅜ x 3⅞ in.
(111 x 98 mm)
Verso: Variant design

PROVENANCE: Edmond Fatio, Geneva (his mark lower right); Fatio sale, Geneva, Rauch, 3–4 June 1959, lot 12; New York, William Schab Gallery, *Catalogue No. 33* [1963], no. 137
Purchase, Gift of the Ian Woodner Family Foundation, 1974.605.5

The impressionistic rapidity of this drawing obscures its function. It could be for a painted overdoor, or for the upper part of a chapel decoration.

52a and b Designs for stage sets

(a) Pen, brown ink, with brown and gray wash. 5⅜ x 4 in. (137 x 102 mm). Laid down on heavy paper

(b) Pen, brown ink, with brown and gray wash. 5⁵⁄₁₆ x 4 in. (135 x 102 mm). Laid down on heavy paper
Gift of Cornelius Vanderbilt, 80.3.627, 629

Classed as anonymous until now, these drawings had nevertheless been connected with the author of the Fatio drawings. The brilliance and virtuosity of the other Natali drawings is seen here at its most delicate and refined. The artist used a much finer pen than in any of the other drawings, but continued to combine and recombine all his distinctive motifs: the long barrel vaults seen from below and receding steeply back into space, the arches crowned with their putti and cartouches, and the double columns supporting triumphal arches. All create a very personal vision of architectural poetry.

GIOVANNI PAOLO PANINI
(Piacenza 1691–1765 Rome)

53 Design for the decoration of a palace interior

Pen, brown ink, with gray wash. 11 x 20¼ in. (279 x 514 mm). Vertical crease at center with worm holes along it. Laid down on paper that is pieced together. Torn and abraded
Inscribed in brown ink at lower left, *C.G.P. Pannini F.*; with scale, *palmi romani*

EXHIBITIONS: New York, The Metropolitan Museum of Art, "Ornament Prints and Drawings of the Eighteenth Century," 1960
BIBLIOGRAPHY: C. J. Weinhardt, "Ornament Prints and Drawings of the Eighteenth Century," *The Metropolitan Museum of Art Bulletin* XVIII, 1960, p. 156, repr.; S. Jacob, "Ein Dekorationsprojekt Giovanni Paolo Panninis," *Berliner Museen*, n.s., XXIII, no. 2, 1973, p. 67, fig. 2
Gift of Harry G. Friedman, 57.658.296

Panini, Rome's greatest *vedute* painter, probably studied and worked in Piacenza with Ferdinando Bibiena (see Nos. 9, 10), Giuseppe Natali (see No. 46), and Andrea Galluzzi. He was thus thoroughly steeped in the Emilian tradition of decorative painting.

In Rome by 1711, where he studied with Benedetto Luti until about 1718, Panini was described by a contemporary as already "an excellent master, a notable painter of perspectives, landscapes and architecture, as well as excellent figures" (cited in F. Arisi, *Gian Paolo Panini*, Piacenza, 1961, p. 86). His first recorded work in Rome was the decoration, begun in 1718, of an apartment on the ground floor of the Villa Patrizi near Porta Pia for Cardinal Giovanni Patrizi, papal legate to Ferrara, and his brothers. The villa was badly damaged in the nineteenth century and destroyed completely in 1911. Panini quickly gained a name

as a decorative painter, receiving commissions in the next seven years for the decoration of rooms in the Palazzo de Carolis (later the Camera Apostolica), the Seminario Romano (both destroyed), the Quirinal Palace, and for the gallery of Palazzo Alberoni (now removed to the Palazzo Madama).

The interior represented in our drawing has four bays, in one of which is a doorway. At the far right is the end wall, which also contains a doorway. The walls are decorated with illusionistic colonnades, in front of which are portrait busts on pedestals, which themselves may be illusionistic. This drawing does not conform to any of the existing rooms that Panini painted. It is, however, typical of Panini's early style of draughtsmanship of 1718–25, and is close to a drawing in the Kunstbibliothek, Berlin, for a wall decoration that Sabine Jacob associated with Panini's work for the Quirinal Palace ("Ein Dekorationsprojekt Panninis," fig. 1). Jacob distinguished in both works a combination of Roman baroque motifs with Emilian decoration. It may be that the Metropolitan drawing was for one of the many rooms in the Villa Patrizi that Panini designed from 1718 until 1725; but without a clear description of the villa, this remains an hypothesis.

The inscription is puzzling in that while the letter *C* before Panini's name must stand for *Cavaliere*, the artist was named a *Cavaliere dello Sperone d'oro* only in October 1749 (Arisi, *Gian Paolo Panini*, p. 102). Arisi showed that the spelling *Pannini* was a corrupted inscription identifying the artist, rather than a signature, as all of his known signatures read simply *Panini*. For example, when in 1756 Panini was named Secretary of the Accademia di S. Luca, he signed the registers *Panini*, as he had in 1719 when he presented his first painting as a member of the academy (ibid., pp. 87, 103). This explains the discrepancy between the drawing style typical of Panini's early period and the inscription that dates the drawing after 1749.

VINCENZO DAL RÈ
(Parma about 1700–1762 Naples)

54 Design for a church ceiling

Pen, brown ink, with brown, gray, and colored wash. 12 x 17½ in. (305 x 445 mm). Brown ink border on the drawing
Signed in brown ink on a plaque within the design, *Vincenzo Rè Inventore, e delineatore*

PROVENANCE: Edmond Fatio, Geneva (his mark lower right); Fatio sale, Geneva, Rauch, 3–4 June 1959, lot 215, repr., New York, William Schab Gallery, *Catalogue No. 42*, n.d., no. 165, repr.
EXHIBITIONS: Zurich, Graphische Sammlung der Eidgenössische Technische Hochschule in Zürich, *Architektur und Dekorations-Zeichnungen der Barockzeit aus der Sammlung Edmond Fatio, Genf*, 1946, no. 41, repr.;

Florence, La Strozzina, *I Disegni Scenografi della Raccolta Fatio,* 1958, no. 65, fig. 10
The Elisha Whittelsey Collection, The Elisha Whittelsey Fund, 69.590

Emilian by birth, Vincenzo dal Rè was a pupil of the great stage designer Pietro Righini, with whom he worked in Turin and then followed to Naples to assist in the inauguration of the Teatro San Carlo in 1737. Vincenzo succeeded Righini the following year as Royal Theater Architect and Scenographer. He is best known for his stage designs (some very beautiful examples of which were recently on the New York market, [William Schab Gallery, *Catalogue No. 50,* n.d., nos. 71–74, two repr.]), and for his decorations in 1747 for the festivities for the birth of the Duke of Calabria, the son of Charles III, Bourbon king of the Two Sicilies and later King of Spain. These decorations were immortalized in the magnificent book, *Narrazione delle Solenni Reali feste fatte celebrare in Napoli ... per la Nascita del suo primogenito Filippo Real Principe delle Due Sicilie,* published in Naples the following year, for which Vincenzo prepared the drawings for the engravers.

He designed frescoed wall decoration as well, the most famous example of which is for the royal palace at Portici where his painted architectural perspectives enhance the grand entrance staircase (the *scalone*), and several anterooms. A drawing for the decoration of the ceiling of the *scalone* is in the Museo di Capodimonte, Naples (published by F. Mancini, *Scenografia Napoletana dell'Età Barocca,* Naples [1964], p. 105, fig. 47). This drawing shares with ours, in addition to the ornamental style, the contrast of the sprightly draughtsmanship and flickering chiaroscuro to the measured hatching. It too, is signed not in script, but in block printing, as were the stage drawings recently on the New York art market (one of which was signed with a printed monogram).

Represented in this drawing is half of a proposed design for a church ceiling. In the medallions, the following scenes from the Passion are represented: from left to right, the Agony in the Garden, the Kiss of Judas, Christ at the Column, the Crowning with Thorns, and the Ecce Homo. Appropriately, the Crucifix—the central symbol of the Passion—is depicted in the central panel. It is not known for which church this drawing was made, but most likely it was Neapolitan.

GIOVANNI NICCOLÒ SERVANDONI
(Florence 1695–1766 Paris)

55 Design for the garden façade of a palace

Pen, gray ink, with wash. 16⅝ x 32⅞ in. (422 x 835 mm). Paper pieced together from two sheets at left. Originally pasted down on cardboard, now removed

Inscribed in brown ink at top, *Elevation du costé des jardins*; at lower left, *Second projet fait à Paris 1744/ Le Chev Servandoni*; scale at bottom and measurements at right

EXHIBITIONS: New York, The Metropolitan Museum of Art, "Ornament Prints and Drawings of the Eighteenth Century," 1960
BIBLIOGRAPHY: C. J. Weinhardt, "Ornament Prints and Drawings of the Eighteenth Century," *The Metropolitan Museum of Art Bulletin* XVIII, 1960, p. 149, repr.
Gift of the Estate of Ogden Codman, 51.644.151

Servandoni was a pupil and assistant of Panini (No. 53) and of the architect Giuseppe Ignazio Rossi in Rome about 1720. He had, by 1724, established himself in Paris, where he soon succeeded Jean Berain the younger as chief designer for the Royal Opera. His best known work is the façade of St. Sulpice, Paris (designed 1732, later modified); what has been termed its sober classicism is generally considered to have been influential in the development of neoclassicism later in the century. In his theatrical work, which contrasted strikingly with his architecture, Servandoni had immense influence in France as the main interpreter of the grandiose Italian baroque tradition, and especially of the Bibienas. He traveled widely throughout Europe as a stage and festival designer, visiting London, Dresden, Brussels, Vienna, and Stuttgart.

The garden façade of a palace or country château represented in this drawing is typical of the restrained classical idiom of Servandoni's non-theatrical architecture. The precise measurements on the right side indicate that this was a project nearing realization, and was probably executed. It has not been possible to identify this palace or the arms, an oval escutcheon, surmounted by a crown and with griffin supports placed above the arcaded wings between the two end pavilions: Servandoni's work for St. Sulpice and the theater have been extensively studied to the neglect of his domestic architecture.

FRANCESCO STAGNI
(died Bologna 1830)

56 Design for painted wall decoration

Pen, brown and gray ink, with colored wash. 17⁵⁄₁₆ x 12¹⁵⁄₁₆ in. (440 x 329 mm). Laid down

PROVENANCE: Edmond Fatio, Geneva (his mark lower right); Fatio sale, Geneva, Rauch, 3–4 June 1959, lot 226 (one of two drawings)
EXHIBITIONS: Florence, La Strozzina, *I Disegni Scenografi della Raccolta Fatio, 1958,* no. 27; W. R. Jeudwine and Yvonne ffrench, *Exhibition of Old Master Drawings of Stage Designs, Architecture-Ornament,* London, Alpine Club Gallery, 1960, no. 48 or 52
Anonymous Gift, 67.843

Francesco Stagni was a Bolognese painter of *quadratura* and ornament, son of the sculptor and *stuccatore* of the same name (died 1768), with whom he is sometimes confused. This drawing shows clearly the appearance of his frescoes, which decorate many Bolognese palazzi, among them the Palazzo Ferretti-Cospi and the Palazzo Isolani. These scenes were painted on the wall in *quadri riportati* fashion. Classical ruins, represented here in hodge-podge variety, were still a favorite subject for painted interior decoration in the last quarter of the eighteenth century when this drawing must have been made.

The Kunstbibliothek in Berlin has two drawings from the Fatio collection (lot 227 in the Rauch sale) inscribed with Stagni's name on the verso (Hdz 6965, 6966). Their style is compatible with that of this drawing, supporting its traditional attribution.

MAURO ANTONIO TESI
(Modena 1730–1766 Bologna)

57 Design for an altar erected for Holy Week

Pen, brown ink, with brown wash. 7⅜ x 4⅝ in.
(187 x 118 mm). Formerly laid down on paper with a partial Gothic A stamped in purple ink

PROVENANCE: Janos Scholz, New York
The Elisha Whittelsey Collection, The Elisha Whittelsey Fund, 52.570.336

Mauro Tesi, who died at the age of 36, enjoyed great fame for one so young. His talent is demonstrated in brilliant drawings such as this one. This drawing was identified by Richard Wunder as the design for the etching, plate 12 of *Raccolta di Disegni Originali di Mauro Tesi estratti da diverse collezioni . . .* by Count Massimiliano Gini under the pseudonym of Ludovico Inig, (Bologna, 1787). Tesi's biographer, Luigi Crespi, related that Tesi was from a poor Modenese family, and taught himself by copying the drawings and the painted works of the great Bolognese masters of *quadratura* of the previous century, Agostino Mitelli and Angelo Michele Colonna. All kinds of ornament interested Tesi, but soon a natural predisposition towards architectural decoration asserted itself. He decorated many chapels throughout Bologna and worked in Florence, in Pistoia with Antonio Bibiena on the construction of a new theater and its sets, and in Pisa where he designed, with Carlo Bianconi (Nos. 5–8), the monument to Count Francesco Algarotti (died 1764). This monument to his friend and benefactor was finally erected in the Campo Santo after Tesi's death in 1766. Tesi was so esteemed by his fellow artists that they erected a monument to him in S. Petronio, the cathedral of Bologna.

The inscription on the etching after this drawing identifies it as *Prima Idea d'una machina sepolcrale da erigersi per la Settimana Santa nella Chiesa di S. Maria del Bara-* *cano. Il disegno è posseduto dal Sig. Salvatore Dotti.* There are two further designs for the project published in the *Raccolta,* both less graceful and rather heavier in form than this almost evanescent drawing. Count Gini related in the introduction of the *Raccolta,* which is a biography of Tesi, that in 1765 Tesi designed for Holy Week an elegant and beautiful structure in S. Maria del Baracano that was much admired throughout Bologna. It was in S. Maria del Baracano that Tesi was buried the following year.

58 Design for an altar

Pen, deep brown ink, with wash. 5⁹⁄₁₆ x 2⅜ in.
(141 x 60 mm). Laid down on blue paper

PROVENANCE: Janos Scholz, New York
The Elisha Whittelsey Collection, The Elisha Whittelsey Fund, 52.570.209

Richard Wunder identified this drawing as by Tesi. It is close in spirit and handling to the free and dashing theater drawings for which Tesi is better known (see, for example, Portsmouth, 1969, no. 58, repr.). The hand is very fluid, drawing in circular movements, except for the fine, quick hatching. This contrasts with the nervous, scratchy style of No. 57, which might not be so readily connected with Tesi were it not for the etching identifying it.

Tesi's great range as a designer is illustrated by the wide variety of subjects in the *Raccolta:* stage sets, landscapes, palace façades, altars, and festival architecture. His drawing style varies: sometimes tight and precise, capable of rendering delicate neoclassic ornament, and other times sweeping and evocative.

In complete contrast are his early drawings for the Accademia Clementina (now in the Accademia di Belle Arti, Bologna), dated 1748 and 1749, when he was in his late teens. One is for a church façade, the other an altar; the former, especially, is confused in its architectural rendering, which is heavy and densely packed with ornament. The drawing style shows hints of his later fluidity, but is essentially awkward and provincial. That the same artist later created our drawing reveals the brilliant talent that earned Tesi such great renown in his lifetime.

GIOVANNI ANTONIO TORRICELLI
(attributed to)
(Lugano 1716–after 1781 North Italy)

59 Design for a cupola decoration

Pen, brown ink, with gray, brown, and colored wash.
12¼ x 12¼ in. (311 x 311 mm). A Gothic A stamped in purple ink upper left
Inscribed in brown ink at lower left, *Toricelli*

Giovanni Antonio and his twin brother Giuseppe (1716–1808) often collaborated on interior painted decoration, Giuseppe painting the figures, Giovanni Antonio the architectural ornament. They are reported to have studied in Bologna and then to have worked in the principal cities of Italy before they went abroad. Their works are documented in southern Germany in the 1740s and their great work was the painting in the upper choir at Einsiedeln (where the more famous German rococo painters, the Asam brothers, were responsible for the principal decoration). After working in Lucerne, they returned to Lugano, where they painted a ceiling in the cathedral of S. Lorenzo. Thereafter, they worked in Turin, Milan, Como, and Bergamo.

The attribution here depends solely on the inscription. However, since the drawing is typical of the kind of painted ceiling decoration practiced in Piedmont and Lombardy in the third quarter of the eighteenth century, and as it is from a hand of artistic authority, it seems best to leave it as the work of Torricelli, whose drawings are not otherwise known.

LUIGI VANVITELLI
(Naples 1700–1773 Caserta)

60 Design for the altar of the Cappella della Madonna in S. Ciriaco, Ancona

Pen, brown ink, over black chalk. 17 x 11⅜ in.
(432 x 289 mm). Watermark: fleur-de-lys in double circle surmounted by a *V*, near Heawood 1591
Inscribed in brown ink at lower right, *Capella delle Reliquie di S. Ciriaco d'Ancona*; scale at bottom

Luigi Vanvitelli, son of a Dutch view painter who italianized his name after settling in Italy, was trained by his father in Rome, after the family moved from Naples. His talent as a figural draughtsman may be seen in many of his drawings preserved at the royal palace at Caserta. Little is known of his youthful architectural training: it is said that he studied with Juvarra, but this is unlikely, as Juvarra left Rome in 1714 and only returned there for short visits. There is evidence, however, of at least one meeting between the two. In 1732 Vanvitelli's architectural personality clearly emerged when he entered the most important architectural competition of the period, that for the façade of S. Giovanni in Laterano, organized by Pope Clement

XII. Vanvitelli lost to the Florentine Alessandro Galilei, but his design, along with that of Nicola Salvi, was cited for its distinction. Clement soon named Vanvitelli papal architect for the Marches; most of his activity for the next decade and a half was centered there, although he produced some notable works in Rome. In 1750, Vanvitelli was appointed architect to the king of Naples, Charles III, who planned an enormous royal palace at Caserta, outside Naples. Vanvitelli moved to Naples and began the palace that was to become the most important eighteenth-century architectural undertaking in Southern Italy. The huge palace at Caserta, containing over 1,200 rooms, was finished a year after Vanvitelli's death. Conceived on a strict grid plan, the palace consists of four interlocking rectangles. Its classical façade in no way indicates the treatment of the interior: the magnificent staircase is fully in the baroque tradition, and the arches of the octagonal vestibules produce elaborate scenographic effects of rich, multiple views. While working on Caserta, Vanvitelli designed many churches, palazzi, and villas in Naples and its surroundings.

The Metropolitan Museum has the largest known collection of Vanvitelli drawings outside Naples and Caserta, as Jörg Garms has pointed out (Naples, 1973, p. 7). All of our Vanvitelli drawings, both autograph and studio, are exhibited here.

The Cappella della Madonna was only one of the numerous works executed by Vanvitelli in Ancona: he worked on the engineering of the port (the most important on the Adriatic after Venice), designed the Lazzaretto, or quarantine hospital, and the classical Arco Clementino, both in the port area, and redesigned the church of the Gesù and the convent of S. Agostino (See L. Serra, "Le fabbriche di Luigi Vanvitelli in Ancona," *Dedalo* II, 1929–30, pp. 98–110).

S. Ciriaco is the cathedral of Ancona. The raised and deeply set back Cappella della Madonna, formerly called delle Reliquie, is situated to the left of the crossing. As part of the fervent archaeological purism of the late nineteenth century, the chapel was stripped of all its baroque and later decoration, leaving a drearily uninspired and incorrect version of the original romanesque. Vanvitelli's altar was spared, but his entrance was destroyed. The freestanding altar, erected in 1738–39 for Cardinal Bartolommeo Massei, is simple in overall outline, but rich in ornamentation and combination of colored marbles. Two urns probably surmounted the ends of the balustrade, replaced in the nineteenth century by four angels who held aloft a cartouche with the initials of the Virgin above the center of the altar (now removed; ibid., pp. 103–105, repr.). Our drawing obviously does not indicate these angels, and has a simple curved bracket instead of the more elaborate volute that terminates the balustrade that surmounts the altar and also supports the urns. No. 60 must be a preliminary sketch for

43

the altar as it differs from the altar as erected. It contains Vanvitelli's indications of the decoration of the chapel, visible behind the oval altar, as well as a partial ground plan of the altar. Our drawing thus documents the lost baroque decoration of the chapel.

Vanvitelli mentioned another drawing of the altar, whose location is now unknown, when he wrote to his brother in 1751 that he had received a sack of twenty pounds of the finest coffee from the bishop of Ancona in recompense for a drawing of the altar of the Cappella delle Reliquie of S. Ciriaco which "I made for him last year," long after the altar was in place (F. Strazzullo, "I primi anni di Luigi Vanvitelli a Caserta," *Archivio storico di Terra di Lavoro* III, 1964, p. 454).

61 Design for an altar

Pen, brown ink, with gray wash, over graphite.
12⅝ x 14¹¹⁄₁₆ in. (321 x 373 mm). Vertical crease at left of center. Stained and foxed. Watermark (difficult to decipher): *P* surmounting a circle (?)

PROVENANCE: Sale, Berlin, Galerie G. Bassenge, *Auktion,* 7 November 1967, lot 547
The Elisha Whittelsey Collection, The Elisha Whittelsey Fund, 68.725.2

This drawing and No. 60, formerly attributed to Filippo Juvarra, are typical of Vanvitelli's draughtsmanship. The misattribution is not unusual, as Vanvitelli's draughtsmanship, especially in his early drawings and stage designs, is very close to Juvarra's.

The basic design of this unidentified tabular altar is blocked out in graphite; there are alternate suggestions on either side of the vertical crease. The main decorative features were quickly sketched in pen and ink: the curved brackets with pendant garlands, the tabernacle embellished with putto heads, the oval medallion, and the niche containing a chalice.

62 Detail study for the façade of Milan cathedral

Pen, gray ink, over graphite. 11¼ x 16¾ in.
(286 x 426 mm). Torn, foxed. Squared, with scale at bottom. Watermark: fleur-de-lys in double circle surmounted by a *V*, near Heawood 1591

PROVENANCE: Edmond Fatio, Geneva (his mark lower right); Fatio sale, Geneva, Rauch, 3–4 June 1959, lot 242; Donald Oenslager, New York
Gift of Donald Oenslager, 65.536.5

In 1745, Vanvitelli was called to Milan to submit a design for the façade of Milan cathedral. Since the fourteenth century, numerous projects had been designed for it, but none

executed. In 1733, Juvarra submitted two designs, neither of which could be agreed upon. He left for Spain two years later, and was succeeded by Nicola Salvi. Vanvitelli was called in when Salvi withdrew for reasons of health after six years of work.

Vanvitelli's presentation design is preserved in the Archivio della Fabbrica del Duomo, Milan (K. Noehles, "I vari atteggiamenti nel confronto del gotico nei disegni per la facciata del Duomo di Milano," *Il Duomo di Milano, Congresso Internazionale, Atti,* I, 1968, pp. 159–167, fig. 2; see also R. Wittkower, *Gothic vs. Classic: Architectural Projects in Seventeenth-Century Italy,* New York, 1974, pp. 24, 25, 61, 62).

Our drawing, a fully evolved study of the lower level of the façade, is squared for transfer and agrees in every respect with Vanvitelli's finished drawing. A ground plan at the bottom of the Milan sheet shows that the twisted columns stand away from the façade, forming a portico of Gothic arches. Within them the existing classical doors and windows, clearly defined in ink in our drawing, are retained.

Nino Carboneri recently observed that Vanvitelli's lower story is based on the model of 1648 by Francesco Castelli (cited by Noehles, "I vari atteggiamenti," p. 164); it was only in the high, upper level that Vanvitelli demonstrated an original and ingenious solution. A vivid sketch by Vanvitelli in the Albertina, Vienna (ibid., figs. 1, 4; see also K. Noehles, "I progetti del Vanvitelli e del Vittone per la facciata del Duomo di Milano," *Arte in Europa: Scritti di Storia dell'arte in onore di Edoardo Arslan,* I, 1966, pp. 869–874, figs. 585, 586) has on its verso a partial side view of the façade that shows the deep portico and the extremely high upper story looming above the existing Gothic structure of the cathedral. Although Vanvitelli may have derived details of his façade from Castelli, Noehles has shown that the geometrical proportions of his entire scheme are based on Cesare Cesariano's illustrations using Milan cathedral in his edition of Vitruvius published in Como in 1521. A large study for one of the twisted columns is preserved in the royal palace at Caserta (Naples, 1973, no. 115; de' Seta, *Vanvitelli,* no. 97, repr.).

Vanvitelli's façade was harshly criticized for its combination of Gothic and "Greek" elements (as his critics termed them). A bitter controversy followed its rejection.

63 Design for the chair of the statue of St. Peter

Pen, brown ink, over graphite. 14⁷⁄₁₆ x 10⅛ in.
(367 x 257 mm). Horizontal crease below center

PROVENANCE: Paul Fatio, Geneva (his mark lower right); sale, Geneva, Rauch, *Dessins Anciens,* 18–19 June 1962, lot 340

BIBLIOGRAPHY: Garms, 1971, p. 229, note 19
Rogers Fund, 62.129.3

In 1754 the new chair for the bronze statue in St. Peter's replaced an earlier one judged inadequate. The new chair, based on this design, was executed in bardiglio, a blue and white streaked marble (see R. Berliner, "Le Sedie Settecentesche della statua di S. Pietro nella basilica Vaticana," *Studi Romani* IV, 1956, pp. 301–309; Garms, 1971, p. 229; R. Pane, *Vanvitelli*, pp. 83, 84). Vanvitelli sent drawings from Caserta, where he was occupied with the building of the royal palace, to Rome, where the execution of the chair was supervised by his assistant, Carlo Marchionni (Nos. 38, 39). The sculpture itself was by Domenico Giovannini, Vanvitelli's head sculptor at Caserta, who was sent to Rome to work on this project.

The small model for the chair in the Archivio della Fabbrica di S. Pietro (Pane, *Vanvitelli*, figs. 208, 209) closely follows our drawing, except for the addition of a putto's head above St. Peter. Vanvitelli's conception was based principally on Bernini's monumental shrine, the *Cathedra Petri*, and was thus an allusion to the relic of the original chair of the apostle that is contained in the *Cathedra*. Vanvitelli's chair depended on Bernini especially in the high back surmounted by an elliptical C-scroll and in the angels at either side of the chair.

The general reaction to Vanvitelli's chair was adverse. Berliner attributed this to the fact that the statue of St. Peter was raised too high, and worshippers could no longer touch his foot in veneration. Pane considered this unlikely since it is known from one of Vanvitelli's letters that he carefully considered all measurements, including the height of the base. Pane saw its rejection rather as dissatisfaction with the strident contrast of the rigid and archaic statue and the rich, baroque chair. Vanvitelli's chair was replaced two years later by one in a *quattrocento* style that is still in place today. Berliner published a print by G. B. Sintes of 1727 that showed that the original chair was very close to the one now seen in St. Peter's ("Le Sedie Settecentesche," p. 308, pl. 57). A drawing in the Cooper-Hewitt Museum by Vanvitelli of St. Peter's chair strikingly resembles the present one in St. Peter's (acc. no. 1938–88–8570; see Elaine Evans Dee, *The Two Sicilies* [exhibition catalogue], Finch College Museum of Art, New York, no. 52, repr.). It is probably Vanvitelli's own record of the original chair which he used before making the design here exhibited.

64 Design for the high altar of the Gesù Nuovo, Naples

Black chalk and graphite. 20¼ x 14⁹⁄₁₆ in. (514 x 379 mm). Horizontal crease at center. Foxed. Scale at bottom. Watermark: fleur-de-lys in double circle surmounted by a *V*, near Heawood 1591

PROVENANCE: Edmond Fatio, Geneva (his mark lower right); Fatio sale, Geneva, Rauch, 3–4 June 1959, lot 242; Donald Oenslager, New York
Gift of Donald Oenslager, 65.536.2

The Jesuit symbol surmounting this altar identifies the order for which it was designed. On 26 April 1753, Vanvitelli wrote his brother that the Provost of the Gesù Nuovo, one of Naples' major Jesuit churches, "vuole accomodare l'altare maggiore, onde bisognerà che io prenda le misure. Egli dice volere una cosa magnifica. . . ." (F. Strazzullo, "I primi anni di Luigi Vanvitelli a Caserta," *Archivio Storico di Terra di Lavoro* III, 1964, p. 484; Garms, 1971, pp. 212, 213). The word *accomodare* has several English meanings: to repair, adjust, put in order, adorn, and put up. Since Vanvitelli mentioned that he intended to take measurements and that the provost wanted something magnificent, he surely intended to do more than simply repair the altar.

The history of the Gesù Nuovo high altar is unclear: it seems to have been designed in the seventeenth century by Cosimo Fanzago (1591–1678), a Neopolitan baroque architect and sculptor, to replace one burned in 1639 (on the Gesù Nuovo see M. Errichetti in *Societas, Rivista dei Gesuiti dell' Italia Meridionale*, 1959, pp. 33 ff.). However, Fanzago died before completion of the altar, and his plans were so changed that the design of the altar was no longer considered his. The altar was nearing completion in 1724, when Carlo Celano described it in the second edition of his *Notizie della città di Napoli*. He wrote in the third edition in 1758 that the altar was finished and that it contained a rich silver statue of the Virgin of the Immaculate Conception. Celano, surprisingly, made no mention of alterations by Vanvitelli, who was then certainly the most important architect in Naples. The last change was made in 1857, when the wooden altar table was replaced by one in rich marble to conform to the rest of the high altar.

Our drawing—except for those areas Vanvitelli had not yet sketched in—presents nearly the same aspect as the high altar seen today in the Gesù Nuovo. The most notable difference between our drawing and the present altar is a change in the curved pediment derived from Borromini. The basic composition is the same: six engaged half columns supporting a pediment, with a niche at center containing pilasters echoing the half columns. The scale and measurements on the drawing were carefully made in accordance with a working drawing.

65 Design for a church interior

Pen, brown ink, over graphite. 15⅞ x 20½ in. (403 x 521 mm). Vertical crease at center. Foxed. Watermark: fleur-de-lys in double circle surmounted by a *V*, near Heawood 1591

PROVENANCE: Edmond Fatio, Geneva (his mark lower right); Fatio sale, Geneva, Rauch, 3–4 June 1959, lot 242; Donald Oenslager, New York
Gift of Donald Oenslager, 65.536.3

This longitudinal section of a small church with only three bays contains the arms of the Albani family (three monticules and a star) in the coffers of the vault at lower left. Cardinal Annibale Albani, nephew of Pope Clement XI, gave Vanvitelli some of his first commissions. In 1728–29 Vanvitelli worked on the decoration of Cardinal Albani's palace in Urbino (for a drawing by Vanvitelli, see Garms in Naples, 1973, no. 55, repr.). Vanvitelli remained active in the service of Cardinal Albani, as his many drawings with Albani arms attest, but only that for the palace at Urbino has been connected with a known building.

Our drawing has not been identified, but Garms has kindly pointed out its similarity to that for Vanvitelli's first project for the interior of the small church in Pesaro, S. Maria Maddalena (ibid., no. 99, repr.). Vanvitelli designed in the mid-1740s the interior of this church built on a Greek-cross plan by Antonio Rinaldi. The Albani arms make little sense in the context of a Pesaro church, Garms noted, except that Vanvitelli was a close friend of one of Pesaro's most distinguished citizens, Annibale Abbati Olivieri, a distant cousin of Cardinal Albani, who was close to the family (letter from Vanvitelli to Olivieri cited by Garms in Naples, 1973, no. 55).

66 Design for a theater interior

Pen, brown ink, over graphite. 11¼ x 16⅞ in. (286 x 429 mm). Slightly foxed

PROVENANCE: Edmond Fatio, Geneva (his mark lower right); Fatio sale, Geneva, Rauch, 3–4 June 1959, lot 242; Donald Oenslager, New York
Gift of Donald Oenslager, 65.536.1

This is a spirited sketch for the upper-tier boxes of a theater. It is possible that Nos. 66 and 67 are related, as they both share the same provenance, and since No. 67 verso is the sketch for a theater ground plan.

The ceiling here is indicated above the main box, which is set off by what appear to be double columns or pilasters. Vanvitelli's ideas for this theater were sufficiently advanced for him to suggest furnishings: for example, the lanterns and curtains for the boxes.

67 Design for a doorway and wall decoration

Pen, gray ink, over black chalk. 11 x 16⅝ in. (279 x 422 mm). Foxed. Scale at bottom
Verso: Ground plan of a theater. Black chalk and graphite

PROVENANCE: Edmond Fatio, Geneva (his mark lower right); Fatio sale, Geneva, Rauch, 3–4 June 1959, lot 242; Donald Oenslager, New York
Gift of Donald Oenslager, 65.536.4

The sketch of a horseshoe-shaped theater on the verso is probably connected with the theater interior on No. 66. It may also identify the recto of this sheet as the entrance to the boxes of the theater. The curtain seen through the doorway is difficult to explain except as the curtain for the interior of a theater box similar to those depicted in No. 66.

This design for a wall scheme whose principal component is a doorway—two alternate studies are at left—otherwise resembles many palace interiors decorated by Vanvitelli. It would probably be intended for illusionistic painted decoration in such a palace interior. The painted columns would have framed a decorative scheme, perhaps a view of ruins, such as No. 56 by Stagni. Similar interiors by Vanvitelli are seen, for example, in drawings for his elegant rococo decorations for Palazzo Sciarra, Rome (Naples, 1973, nos. 77–84, some repr.; see also L. Salerno, "Inediti di Luigi Vanvitelli e del Pannini: L'Appartamento Settecentesco di Palazzo Sciarra," *Palladio* IX, 1965, pp. 4–8).

Our drawing closely resembles one at Caserta (Naples, 1973, no. 95, repr.), in which the design combines a doorway pediment quite similar to that depicted at lower left in our drawing but with an oval medallion similar to that of the principal doorway at right. The doorway's position between columns is also similar to ours. The Caserta drawing is, however, much livelier: Vanvitelli's nervous pen quickly sketched in the design, whereas our drawing's scheme was carefully set down in black chalk over which the penwork was almost routinely added. Garms connected the Caserta drawing to two others (ibid., nos. 93, 94, repr.) which he dated to the 1730s.

68 Design for a fountain

Pen, brown ink, with gray wash, over traces of black chalk. 6⅜ x 9¾ in. (164 x 247 mm). Inlaid into modern paper

Verso: Stage design. Pen, brown ink, traces of red chalk, with gray wash
Inscribed, *V.S.* [the rest of the line canceled as are the following four; inscription resumes at the end of line six] *possa adempire/ qualche suo commando che anzioso l'attendo per dimos[strare?]/ quanto sia la stima che faccio di un mio padrone al qu[ale]/ mi gli dedico [al suo merito con ossequio*—canceled] */ La Stimatissima di V.S./ Luigi Van . . . t*

PROVENANCE: S. Kaufman, London
EXHIBITIONS: Portsmouth, 1969, no. 103, repr.
Harris Brisbane Dick Fund and Joseph Pulitzer Bequest, 1971.513.22

The scheme of the stage design on the verso, a grand staircase flanked by a giant order of columns leading behind to another set of stairs in a large vestibule, somewhat resembles two other drawings by Vanvitelli at Caserta (Naples, 1973, no. 24, repr.; see also de' Seta, *Vanvitelli*, nos. 18a, 19a, repr.). Kaufman and Knox in the Portsmouth catalogue associated certain architectural components in this drawing with Juvarra, as did Garms in discussing the Caserta drawing (Naples, 1973, no. 24, repr.). As has been observed (No. 61), Vanvitelli's early drawings and those for stage sets come closer to Juvarra's in their architectural motifs and draughtsmanship.

Kaufman and Knox connected the fountain on the recto with Vanvitelli's design for the Fontana di Eolo in the park at Caserta. They also noted Juvarra's influence here, and mentioned similar designs for fountains by Juvarra, the closest of which is in the Biblioteca Nazionale, Turin (Riserva 59-4, leaf 65, no. 5; Rovere, Viale, Brinckmann, pl. 179; Messina, 1966, fig. 43). A more telling comparison is with some of Vanvitelli's own fountain designs that are parts of garden stage sets (Naples, 1973, nos. 17, 18, repr.). The treatment of our drawings and those at Caserta is similar; all three seem to date from the same period. Garms dated the garden stage set drawings to Vanvitelli's first period, about 1720–32. As an early date is also appropriate for the verso, it is unlikely that the fountain is the design for that at Caserta, although it does present certain similarities with it. Garms noted that in some of Vanvitelli's drawings it is often difficult to tell whether a drawing is for imaginary architecture, such as a stage set, or for an actual structure. Our fountain seems to fit into that category of ambiguous design. However, as the verso is certainly a stage design, the fountain may be one as well.

The attribution of the drawing to Vanvitelli was made by Mercedes Viale Ferrero.

LUIGI VANVITELLI (workshop)

69 Façade decorated for the marriage festivities of the king of Naples

Pen, gray ink, with gray wash. 12½ x 18½ in.
(318 x 470 mm). Laid down and inlaid into modern paper. Torn, with holes and abrasions. Watermark: *D & C Blauw,* near Heawood 3267 right
Inscribed in gray ink below design above plan, *Façade faite au Palais ou on avoit disposée la Sale du Bal, par ordre de Monsr de Kaunitz, pour le Mariage du Roy de Naples, avec / l'Archiduchesse de Autriche Marie Carlotte.*; at lower left corner, *De Monsr Vanvitelli, Premier Architecte du Roy de Naples.*; scale at bottom, *Echelle de 50 Palm. Napolits*

PROVENANCE: Edward Gordon Craig, London, Paris, and Italy; Edward Craig
The Elisha Whittelsey Collection, The Elisha Whittelsey Fund, 64.669.4

On 7 April 1768, the seventeen-year-old king of Naples, Ferdinando IV, was married by proxy in Vienna to Maria Carolina, archduchess of Austria, daughter of the empress Maria Theresa and sister of Marie Antoinette. Maria Carolina arrived at Caserta in mid-May at which time a month

of festivities began (for Vanvitelli's references in his letters to the celebrations, see Garms, 1971, pp. 220–221, 258). On 12 and 13 June, lavish suppers and a ball were given by the Austrian ambassador, Count Kaunitz, at Prince Teora's palace on the sea at Chiaja near Posillipo. Vanvitelli designed the decorations for these events, and then prepared a manuscript describing the festivities and his decorations. The manuscript is entitled *Narrazione delle feste date in Napoli da S.E., il Sig. Conte Ernesto di Kaunitz Rittberg ... Ambasciadore Straordinario delle SS. MM. Imperiali Reali Apostoliche ... In occasione del sposalizio di S. Mta Ferdinando IV Re delle due Sicilie ... con la Serenissima Altezza Reale Maria Carolina Archiduchessa d'Austria, L'anno MDCCLXVIII* (Naples, Biblioteca Nazionale Ms XV-A-8; see R. Pane, *L'Architettura dell'età barocca in Napoli,* Naples, 1939, pp. 281–282). A printed book was definitely contemplated, as the manuscript ended with cost estimates for printing, binding, and illustrating with engraved copper plates (in a letter of 1768, Vanvitelli mentioned his intention of producing prints illustrating the marriage festivities, see ibid., p. 220; see also L. Vanvitelli [the younger], *Vita dell'Architetto Luigi Vanvitelli,* Naples, 1823, pp. 45–46). On the title page of his manuscript, Vanvitelli drew a cartouche surmounted by a crown (not a royal one, but perhaps for Kaunitz) and on the first page, a large decorated initial, depicting Vesuvius smoking, which is very similar to the initial he designed for the book *Lettere ad un amico ...* (Naples, 1772). The *Lettere* described the festivities given by the duke d'Arcos for the baptism of Ferdinando and Maria Carolina's first-born daughter. Had the marriage *Narrazione* been produced, it surely would have been similar to the *Lettere,* which contained a number of large, full-page engravings.

Our three drawings of the decorations for the marriage festivities (Nos. 69–71) were probably studies drawn by one of Vanvitelli's assistants for the engravings for the intended published version of the *Narrazione.* The French inscriptions suggest that they were possibly made for the Austrian court, where French was a court language. The incorrect French—most accents are omitted—further supports the hypothesis that they were written by an Italian assistant in Vanvitelli's shop. Curiously, the inscription misidentifies the bride as *Marie Carlotte.*

Because Prince Teora's palace was considered too small for the expected crowds, Vanvitelli erected in the garden a large ballroom whose stately exterior is shown in the present drawing. The arms of Austria surmount the balustrade at the center above a Palladian triumphal arch. According to Vanvitelli in the *Narrazione,* the cartouche above the niche within the arch contains a representation of Peace and Justice embracing. However, the two figures are barely discernible in our drawing. The medallions at the ends of the façade above the statues in niches, the artist wrote, contained portraits of the first Austrian emperor, Rudolf I, and the reigning emperor, Joseph II. There is a strong resemblance between the ballroom façade and a design in the Museo di S. Martino, Naples, attributed to Vanvitelli by Paolo Mezzanotte and de' Seta, for the façade of the Palazzo Ducale, Milan (1769), especially in the general proportions, heavy rustication of the first story, and treatment of the fenestration and giant order of columns on the second story that recall Caserta (see P. Mezzanotte, "Il Vanvitelli a Milano," *Atti dell' VIII Convegno Nazionale di Storia dell'Architettura, Caserta, 1953,* Rome, 1956, pp. 92–93, fig. 2; de' Seta, *Vanvitelli,* p. 305, no. 136, repr.). The major differences are the absence of a mezzanine in our drawing and in the main portals and the treatment of the windows above them. There are two portals on the Milan façade, and their windows on the second story are surmounted by triangular pediments. Garms connected another drawing, in the Museo di S. Martino, which he did not consider autograph or even a project by Vanvitelli, with our façade (inv. no. 3325C; Naples, 1973, no. 150). He thought this drawing, which has a central portal in the upper story as does ours, was known to Vanvitelli when planning the façade of the palace at Caserta, or, more likely, the Palazzo Ducale in Milan. Garms cites another drawing for the ballroom façade in the Biblioteca Comunale, Foligno.

70 Ballroom decorated for the marriage festivities of the king of Naples

Pen, gray ink, with gray wash. 11½ x 19¼ in.
(292 x 489 mm). Laid down and inlaid into modern paper. Torn, with abrasions. Watermark: escutcheon containing the letters *D* and *C* above *B*, near Heawood 3267 left
Inscribed in gray ink below design, *Coupe sur la Longueur de la Sale du Bal, disposée par ordre de Monsr de Kaunitz, pour le Mariage du Roy de Naples, avec l'Archiduchesse de Autriche Marie Carlotte;* at lower left corner, *De Monsr Vanvitelli, Premier Architecte du Roy de Naples;* scale at middle right, *Echelle de 50 Palm. Napolit^s*

PROVENANCE: Edward Gordon Craig, London, Paris, and Italy; Edward Craig
The Elisha Whittelsey Collection, The Elisha Whittelsey Fund, 64.669.7

For a discussion of the marriage and Vanvitelli's planned publication, see No. 69.

The scheme of this oval ballroom is similar to a theater. At the sides of the room rose a series of steps, like theater stalls; in fact, Vanvitelli used the word *platea,* Italian for pit and stalls of a theater, to describe the room. Chairs on which the guests sat between dances were placed on the raised steps. This plan resembles that employed by Vanvitelli in 1772 for the celebrations for the birth of the daughter of the king of Naples illustrated in *Lettere ad un amico.*

In the *Narrazione* manuscript, Vanvitelli recounted that many of the flowers and wreaths used in these decorations

were "natural," or fresh. Apollo with his lyre stands on the raised platform at the left, and the royal arms are suspended at both ends of the room.

An important component of the ballroom is the row of slender columns supporting the pointed vaults, which produces an elegantly light effect. The brilliant scheme of candelabra attached to the columns, echoed by the hanging chandeliers that punctuate the spaces between the columns, further enhances the beauty of the ensemble.

71 Ceiling of the ballroom decorated for the marriage festivities of the king of Naples

Pen, gray ink, with gray wash. 13⅛ x 18 in.
(333 x 457 mm). Laid down and inlaid into modern paper. Torn, with abrasions and stains. Watermark: *D & C Blauw,* near Heawood 3267 right
Inscribed in gray ink below design, *Plafond de la Sale du Bal, disposee par ordre de Monsr de Kaunitz, pour le Mariage du Roy de Naples, avec l'Archiduchesse de Autriche Marie Carlotte;* at lower left corner, *Monsr Vanvitelli, Premier Architecte du Roy de Naples.;* scale at bottom, *Echelle de 50 Palm. Napolit^s*

PROVENANCE: Edward Gordon Craig, London, Paris, and Italy; Edward Craig
The Elisha Whittelsey Collection, The Elisha Whittelsey Fund, 64.669.3

For a discussion of the marriage and Vanvitelli's planned publication, see No. 69.

The central panel of the oval ballroom ceiling depicts the Marriage of Cupid and Psyche. The overall classical disposition of the ceiling, divided into curved panels that were probably executed in stucco, demonstrates Vanvitelli's ability to combine disparate styles — the Gothic arches and the classical ceiling — into a unified conception that is wholly personal.

72 Caserta theater, ground plan with ceiling view

Pen, gray ink, with gray wash. 13⅛ x 18 in.
(333 x 457 mm). Laid down and inlaid into modern paper. Torn, with large area missing at upper right, abrasions and some stains. Watermark: *D & C Blauw,* near Heawood 3267 right
Inscribed in gray ink below design, *Plan du petit Theatre & de son Plafond dans le Palais neuf de Caserte x x x x x x.* At bottom left, *... V ...;* scale at middle right, *Echelle de 40 Palm. Napolit^s*

PROVENANCE: Edward Gordon Craig, London, Paris, and Italy; Edward Craig
The Elisha Whittelsey Collection, The Elisha Whittelsey Fund, 64.669.3

The drawings for the Caserta theater (Nos. 72–75) conform in format, draughtsmanship, and inscriptions to those for the marriage celebration of Ferdinando, king of Naples, and Maria Carolina of Austria (Nos. 69–71). Like them, the theater drawings must be studio preparations for engravings. The partially obliterated inscription at the lower left of this drawing can be deciphered as *Vanvitelli Premier Architecte du Roy de Naples,* the same inscription as that on Nos. 69–71. All the theater drawings were, no doubt, similarly signed, but have been cut down. All seven drawings have similar watermarks and must have been drawn on the same size paper, as indicated by the placement of the partial inscription, *du Roy,* on No. 75. It is possible that the theater drawings were planned for publication either with the festival drawings or in a later volume. It is not known when the theater opened, although by Carnival of 1769 "feste grandiose"—spectacular galas—were held in it. (F. Strazzullo, *Autografi vanvitelliani per la reggia di Caserta,* Naples, 1956, p. 24).

In No. 72, the plan of the horseshoe-shaped theater, showing the stage at right with indications of the flats, is combined with a sketch of the ceiling decoration. The ceiling consists of a series of vaults capped by the round central panel in which King Ferdinando is alluded to in the representation of the Apotheosis of Apollo. The painter Crescenzo La Gamba decorated the interior of the theater, and Gaetano Magri painted the ornament. Vanvitelli had summoned both artists to Caserta since he considered the local artists, especially the ornamental painters, not up to his standards. The Caserta theater is imposing, worthy of the magnificent palace of which it is a part.

Other drawings for the Caserta theater are in the Bibliothèque Nationale, Paris (kindly pointed out to me by Jörg Garms), and in the Biblioteca del Istituto di Archeologia e Storia dell'Arte, in Palazzo Venezia, Rome (see A. Rava's review of F. Fichera, *Luigi Vanvitelli,* in *Palladio* III, no. 1, 1939, pp. 44–45, repr.). The position of the theater in the palace is shown in Vanvitelli's folio on Caserta, *Dichiarazione dei Disegni del Reale Palazzo di Caserta . . .* (Naples, 1761), dedicated to Carlo, king of Naples and the Two Sicilies (Ferdinando's father), and to his queen, Maria Amalia. The theater is designated *O* on both the ground plan of the palace, pl. II, and on the section, pl. VIII.

73 Caserta theater, transverse section showing the stage

Pen, gray ink, with gray wash. 11 3/16 x 12 3/4 in. (284 x 324 mm). Laid down and inlaid into modern paper. Torn, with abrasions and some stains. Watermark: *D & C Blauw,* near Heawood 3267 right
Inscribed in graphite at top, *Front*; in gray ink below design, *Coupe sur la Largeur du petit Theatre du Palais de Caserte, qui fait voir la Scene xxx;* scale below, *Echelle de 60 Palm. Napolit*ˢ; evidence of further inscription cut off at bottom

PROVENANCE: Edward Gordon Craig, London, Paris, and Italy; Edward Craig
The Elisha Whittelsey Collection, The Elisha Whittelsey Fund, 64.669.4

Represented on the stage is Dido's immolation scene, possibly from the famous *Dido,* the libretto by Metastasio, which was popular throughout Italy during the mid-eighteenth century. The background consists of a gigantic arcade through the middle arch of which is seen a classical perspective with an obelisk in the center. An autograph Vanvitelli drawing in the Donald Oenslager collection, New York, is considered by Bean and Stampfle to be a design for a stage set at Caserta on the basis of the similarity of its obelisk to that in our drawing (Bean and Stampfle, 1971, no. 172, repr.). In addition, the arcades are strikingly similar.

Strazzullo mentioned that for Carnival of 1770, a production of *Dido* was given in the Caserta theater, followed by a ball (*Autografi vanvitelliani,* p. 24). If our drawing records this production of *Dido,* then perhaps the entire group of drawings here exhibited of the theater and the celebrations of the king's marriage were made more than a year and a half after Vanvitelli wrote the manuscript for his *Narrazione,* dated September 1768.

74 Caserta theater, transverse section showing the royal box

Pen, gray ink, with gray wash. 11 1/4 x 12 3/4 in. (286 x 324 mm). Laid down and inlaid into modern paper. Torn, with abrasions and stains. Watermark: escutcheon containing the letters *D* and *C* above *B,* near Heawood 3267 left
Inscribed in gray ink below design: *Coupe sur la Largeur C D du petit Theatre du Palais de Caserte, qui fait voir la Loge du Roy.*; scale below, *Echelle de 60 Palm. Napolit*ˢ

PROVENANCE: Edward Gordon Craig, London, Paris, and Italy; Edward Craig
The Elisha Whittelsey Collection, The Elisha Whittelsey Fund, 64.669.2

For a discussion of the Caserta theater, see Nos. 72 and 73.

75 Caserta theater, longitudinal section

Pen, gray ink, with gray wash. 12 x 12 1/8 in. (305 x 308 mm). Laid down and inlaid into modern paper. Torn, with holes, abrasions, and stains. Watermark: escutcheon containing the letters *D* and *C* above *B,* near Heawood 3267 left
Inscribed in gray ink below design, *Coupe sur la Longueur A B du petit Theatre du Palais de Caserte x x x x;* at bottom left, *du Roy de Naples;* scale above, *Echelle de 60 Palm. Napolit*ˢ

PROVENANCE: Edward Gordon Craig, London, Paris, and Italy; Edward Craig
The Elisha Whittelsey Collection, The Elisha Whittelsey Fund, 64.669.1

For a discussion of the Caserta theater, see Nos. 72 and 73.

CARLO ZUCCHI THE YOUNGER (attributed to)
(Venice? 1728–1795 Russia?)

76 Design for a stage set

Pen, brown ink, with brown and gray wash. 13⅜ x 20⅛ in.
(340 x 511 mm). Watermark: armorial escutcheon with
bend, surmounted by large fleur-de-lys, with no maker's
name, near W. A. Churchill, *Watermarks in Paper . . . in the
XVII and XVIII Centuries . . .*, Amsterdam, 1935, no. 429.
Signed in brown ink at lower left, *C. Zucchi*; inscribed in
brown ink at lower center, *Gran Salla D'Arme* [or *i*]; at
lower right, 9

PROVENANCE: Joseph Stehlin, Charles Stehlin, New
Rochelle, N.Y.
Harris Brisbane Dick Fund, 47.100.3

This drawing is attributed to the Carlo Zucchi who was the
son of the Venetian stage painter, engraver, and etcher
Andrea Zucchi (1679–1740, died in Dresden). Carlo, a
theatrical designer and decorative painter, was active in
Dresden in 1747–48 and in Cracow in 1752. He is little
studied or known—indeed, he was not included in the au-
thoritative *Enciclopedia dello Spettacolo* (Rome, 1954–
68)—but this drawing shows him to be a stage designer
and draughtsman of merit.

The sheet was identified at purchase as by a Carlo Zucchi
of Reggio Emilia (1789–1848), whose work for the stage
is virtually unknown. He reproduced in aquatint the works
of a number of Reggio stage designers: Francesco Fonta-
nesi, Vincenzo Carnevali, and Giovanni Paglia (see Mario
Degani, *Mostra degli scenografi dal XVII al XX secolo*
[exhibition catalogue], Reggio, 1957, p. 31).

The large hall of a palace, decorated with arms, armor,
military trophies, and ancestral portraits for a drama set in
a vaguely Renaissance period, is laid out *per angolo* in the
tradition of Ferdinando Bibiena. The repetition and emphasis on the heavy scroll brackets supporting the ceiling
recalls the work of the influential Emilian stage designer,
Pietro Righini (1683–1742), especially the plates *Reggia
Magnifica* and *Galeria* from the series of Righini's stage
sets engraved and published in Augsburg in the mid-eighteenth century by Martin Engelbrecht as *Theatralische
Veränderungen vorgestellt in einer zu Mayland gehalten
Opera*. Because of the drawing's affinities to the work of
the eighteenth-century Righini, I believe our drawing
must be the work of the eighteenth-century Venetian Carlo
Zucchi, and not the nineteenth-century Emilian Zucchi.

BOLOGNESE
(About 1740–60)

77a, b, and c Designs for painted overdoors

(a) Pen, brown ink, with wash, over traces of black chalk.
5 x 6⅛ in. (127 x 156 mm). Laid down on paper with a

Gothic A stamped in purple ink at lower right corner
Verso: Sketch of marbleized wall. Brown ink

(b) Pen, brown ink, with wash, over traces of black chalk.
5½ x 3⅛ in. (140 x 79 mm). Laid down on paper with a
Gothic A stamped in purple ink at lower left corner
Verso: Sketches. Black chalk

(c) Pen, brown ink, with wash, over traces of black chalk.
4½ x 5 in. (114 x 127 mm). Laid down on paper with a
Gothic A stamped in purple ink at lower left corner
Verso: Part of a doorway. Brown ink and wash

PROVENANCE: Janos Scholz, New York
The Elisha Whittelsey Collection, The Elisha Whittelsey
Fund, 52.570.144, 145, 146

Bolognese painted wall decoration employed large cartouches sometimes containing landscape scenes, embedded
in rich and profuse architectural ornament. The scheme
spread all over Italy, especially into Piedmont and Lombardy, but was used with greatest elegance and refinement
in Bologna. These handsome Bolognese examples are close
to the kind of domestic decoration that Vittorio Maria
Bigari (1692–1776) and Stefano Orlandi (1681–1760)
executed in and around Bologna.

NORTH ITALIAN
(1735–1760)

78 Design for a *Theatrum Sacrum*

Pen, brown ink, with brown and gray wash. 17¾ x 12¼ in.
(451 x 311 mm). Laid down. Stained. Gothic A stamped
in purple ink at lower right
Inscribed, verso, in pencil, *A. Pozzo?*

PROVENANCE: Janos Scholz, New York
The Elisha Whittelsey Collection, The Elisha Whittelsey
Fund, 52.570.73

The tentative, though incorrect, identification of Andrea
Pozzo on the verso suggests the source of the idea behind
this design for a religious celebration. In his treatise on
perspective published in Rome, *Perspectiva Pictorum et
Architectorum . . .* (vol. I, 1693; vol. II, 1700), Pozzo reproduced a number of his designs for church decorations.
The closest to our drawing is a three-storied, *tempietto*-like
structure that he designed for Maundy Thursday and Good
Friday in S. Ignazio, Rome (vol. I, fig. 66). Pozzo's design
lacks the decorative rococo flourishes of our sheet, which
are not integral to the architectural design.

The decorative details, treatment of the cartouches, and
urns held by putti, suggest a North Italian origin for this
sheet. There are strong hints of Genoese draughtsmanship
in the treatment of the figures. They reflect the style of an
artist such as Domenico Parodi (1668–1740; see M. Newcome, *Genoese Baroque Drawings*, nos. 120, 121, repr.).

Parodi, according to Soprani-Ratti, designed a number of temporary festival decorations (*Delle Vite de' Pittori, Scultori, ed Architetti Genovesi*, II, Genoa, 1769, pp. 224, 225).

As a result of the greater number of artists traveling during the eighteenth century, there was a greater exchange of artistic styles between the areas they visited. This is especially true in Liguria, Piedmont, Lombardy, and the Veneto. Thus, it is often difficult to identify the precise origin of ornament in these regions.

Our drawing may be a design for the celebration of the feast day of St. Gregory (March 12), as it is he who appears with his attributes of church model, cross, and Holy Dove. The theological virtues appear above: Hope at left, Charity at right, with Faith surmounting the cupola. Like Pozzo's inventions, which were designed, as he said, to fool the eye, this must be for a painted backdrop to be set up in a church. If this structure had been intended as a freestanding construction, the two projecting sets of columns on which Hope and Charity stand would be duplicated on the other side. This would present iconographic problems since the natural complement to the theological virtues would be the four cardinal virtues, who would not fit on the two remaining pairs of columns at the back. Alternate design suggestions are presented in the stairways and in the cartouches below the putti.

PIEDMONTESE
(About 1750–75)

79 Design for altar decorations for a liturgical celebration

Pen, brown ink, with brown and gray wash. 20 x 13⅝ in. (508 x 346 mm). Partially laid down on blue paper. Horizontal crease at center. Many small tears at edges, repaired.
Inscribed, verso, in brown ink at bottom left, [G] *Battista Alberoni fece*; on blue paper backing in black chalk, *Bibiena*

EXHIBITIONS: Philadelphia, 1968, no. 45
The Elisha Whittelsey Collection, The Elisha Whittelsey Fund, 54.586

For many years drawings such as this and No. 80 have been connected with Giuseppe Bibiena. In 1915 Corrado Ricci (*I Bibiena architetti teatrali*, Milan, pl. 79) attributed to Giuseppe a very similar drawing of an altar. That drawing was then in the Chevalley collection, Turin. In a variant of the Chevalley drawing now at the University of Wisconsin, Madison (Philadelphia, 1968, no. 32, repr.) putti carry the symbols of the Passion, lacking in the Chevalley drawing, suggesting that the Wisconsin drawing is connected to an Easter *Theatrum Sacrum*. As architect to the imperial court at Vienna and to many German princes, Giuseppe

often had the task of designing decorations for such ecclesiastical ceremonies. In his *Architetture, e prospettive* he published a number of these decorations representing scenes from Christ's Passion (see No. 13). Drawings like these accordingly have been attached to his name.

However, if one compares these drawings to the various engravings of the *Theatra Sacra* in the *Architetture, e prospettive* one sees in these drawings a highly decorative style verging on the rococo that contrasts with the rigorous, late baroque classicism of Giuseppe's architectonic designs. The style of the drawings is reminiscent of the ornament in the drawing attributed to Torricelli (No. 59), long active in Piedmont, and of other Piedmontese drawings (such as those from the Metropolitan's Dalva scrapbook, see No. 30). Other writers, for instance Kelder in discussing No. 80 (Philadelphia, 1968, no. 33), have previously mentioned the Piedmontese characteristics of these drawings while maintaining the attribution to Giuseppe. I suggest that both Metropolitan drawings, as well as those in the Chevalley and Wisconsin collections, are certainly not by Giuseppe Bibiena, but are probably all by the same hand, and are very likely Piedmontese.

Bolognese painted architectural ornament, whether for the stage, wall decoration, or festivities both sacred and secular, was the foundation for the development of Northern Italian ornament. Bolognese artists worked extensively outside the city, exporting their distinctive style; for example, Giuseppe Bibiena was in Piedmont in 1741 for a short time to design the *quadratura* in the cupola of the imposing Santuario at Mondovì. He returned to Vienna before the architectural decoration was actually executed; the design is his, though probably executed by Felice Biella.

The artist mentioned on this drawing's inscription, Giovanni Battista Alberoni, was a painter of perspective and ornament and assistant to Giuseppe Bibiena. Emilian by birth (born perhaps in Modena), and a member of the Accademia Clementina in Bologna, he worked in Turin and Piedmont in the 1750s and early 1760s (see Baudi di Vesme, *Schede Vesme: L'Arte in Piemonte . . .*, I, Turin, 1963, pp. 9–10). His name was registered among the members of the Compagnia di S. Luca in Turin in 1756 and 1759. Documents show he decorated not only the chapels of a number of Piedmontese churches, but was also active as a designer of festival decoration.

I do not know of any Alberoni drawings to support the drawing's inscription. However, the writer of the inscription must have had in mind the distinctive elements of Alberoni's art: one based solidly on a Bolognese framework, closely associated with the work of Giuseppe Bibiena, and overlaid with the Piedmontese decorative details that surely would have been acquired by Alberoni during his residence of over a decade in the region. These qualities epitomize our drawing and clarify its proper context.

The liturgical celebration represented here is that for the *Quarant'Ore* (Forty Hours) which took place during Lent and whose distinctive feature was the exposition of the Holy Sacrament, usually seen, as here, in front of a glory of radiating beams.

PIEDMONTESE
(About 1750–75)

80 Design for altar decorations for a liturgical celebration

Pen, brown ink, with brown and gray wash. 13³⁄₁₆ x 8¾ in. (335 x 222 mm)

PROVENANCE: Edmond Fatio, Geneva (his mark lower right); Fatio sale, Geneva, Rauch, 3–4 June 1959, lot 31 (one of a pair); sale, London, Christie's, 10 July 1962, lot 99; S. Kaufman, London

EXHIBITIONS: Zurich, Graphische Sammlung der Eidgenössische Technische Hochschule in Zürich, *Architecktur und Dekorations-Zeichnungen der Barockzeit aus der Sammlung Edmond Fatio, Genf*, 1946, no. 64; Florence, La Strozzina, *I Disegni Scenografi della Raccolta Fatio*, 1958, no. 37a; Philadelphia, 1968, no. 33; Portsmouth, 1969, no. 67, repr.
Harris Brisbane Dick Fund and Joseph Pulitzer Bequest, 1971.513.75

The scheme of interlocking hexagons with its consequent screen-like effect underscores not only the theatricality of this design but its very derivation: this drawing reads like a stage backdrop. It is probably by the same artist as No. 79, and also for the *Quarant'Ore.*

PIEDMONTESE
(About 1740–80)

81 Design for a painted illusionistic wall decoration

Pen, brown ink, with gray and yellow wash. 11¼ x 17 in. (286 x 432 mm)
Inscribed with scale at bottom, *Trabucho unno*

PROVENANCE: Leon Dalva, New York, Piedmontese scrapbook
Gift of Leon Dalva, 65.654.38

If only the central portion of this drawing were visible, it might be considered a stage design. The classical ruins visible behind architecture set at angles are derived from the tradition of Ferdinando Bibiena's device for stage sets, the *scena per angolo.* The scale in *trabucchi,* a Piedmontese measurement, as well as the provenance, help to identify the drawing's origin.

There are many other drawings by this artist in the Dalva scrapbook, of which some are altar and chapel de-

signs. The artist was probably from the countryside, as this predominantly gray architectonic design is very different from the lighter, more elegant, and colorful wall decoration common in Turin and, for example, at Stupinigi. The kind of decoration illustrated here is usually associated with the small towns of Northern Piedmont and around Lakes Como and Maggiore.

ROMAN
(First third of the eighteenth century)

82 Design for a temporary structure for a festival celebration

Pen, brown ink, with gray wash. 27⅝ x 11¼ in. (702 x 286 mm). Paper composed of two sheets, joined two-thirds from top. Laid down on similar heavy cream-colored paper

PROVENANCE: Parsons, London; sale, London, Sotheby's, 10 November 1954, lot 32; S. Kaufman, London
EXHIBITIONS: Portsmouth, 1969, no. 65, repr.
Harris Brisbane Dick Fund and Joseph Pulitzer Bequest, 1971.513.11

The event which this large and elaborate apparatus commemorates has not been identified, but as Kaufman and Knox noted in the Portsmouth catalogue, it must be a secular one, for there are no ecclesiastical symbols on the drawing. The base consists of a fortified tower on which stands a statue of Minerva within a colonnaded structure containing a cartouche surmounted by a ducal crown. Above this is a triumphal arch in which a portrait bust is held aloft by two figures. Surrounding the columns of the arch are statues that Kaufman and Knox tentatively identified as the Arts of Painting, Architecture, and Astronomy. Surmounting the whole is a stepped cupola that supports a spiral cupola on the top of which Atlas holds a globe surmounted by Fame. A haloed figure leads a crowned figure up the stepped cupola amidst fighting allegorical figures probably representing the Vices and others in seeming adulation carrying standards. Kaufman and Knox saw the underlying theme of this *apparato* to be that of the Tower of Wisdom (*Turris Sapientiae*), the ascent of which was considered man's highest goal.

This drawing may be Roman, as it comes from the same album of drawings as No. 83. Eighteenth-century Rome saw many festivities embellished with structures such as this, some by the most prominent artists of the day. For example, Panini designed the *apparato* for the celebrations of the marriage of the dauphin in 1745 and then painted the scene as well.

The drawing is certainly not by the same hand, as Kaufman and Knox suggested, as a drawing of a festival decoration in the Cooper-Hewitt Museum (published by

Richard Wunder in *Extravagant Drawings of the Eighteenth Century . . .*, New York, 1962, pl. 8, there wrongly attributed to Juvarra).

ROMAN
(First quarter of the eighteenth century)

83 Design for a *carta gloria*

Pen, brown ink, with brown and yellow wash.
22⅛ x 15⅜ in. (565 x 390 mm)

PROVENANCE: Parsons, London; sale, London, Sotheby's,
10 November 1954, lot 32; S. Kaufman, London
EXHIBITIONS: Portsmouth, 1969, no. 97, repr.
Harris Brisbane Dick Fund and Joseph Pulitzer Bequest,
1971.513.67

A *carta gloria* is the frame for an altar card and this one to be executed in silver gilt is associated with St. John the Evangelist, represented in the cartouche at the top of the frame. His symbol, the eagle, is represented in the cartouche at the bottom.

This drawing and others, originally part of an album bound in vellum, said to date from the early eighteenth century and containing a number of designs for metalwork, were formerly attributed to the Roman goldsmith, Giovanni Giardini (Forlì 1646–1721 Rome). Designer of precious metalwork for the Camera Apostolica, Giardini carried out some of the most important commissions in metal of his time. One of the most unusual of these was a silver mask, crown, and scepter for the remains of Queen Christina of Sweden that were buried with her and only discovered recently when her casket was opened (see A. Lipinsky, "Arte orafa a Roma, Giovanni Giardini da Forlì," *Arte Illustrata* IV, 1971, pp. 18–34; and further, the basic work on Giardini, C. Grigioni, *Giovanni Giardini da Forlì*, Rome, 1963).

Giardini had many of his designs published in *Disegni Diversi inventati e delineati da Giovanni Giardini da Forlì . . . intagliati in Roma da M. G. Limpach*, 1714 (republished in 1750 as *Promptuarium Artis Argentariae*)

for which the Kunstbibliothek in Berlin has a volume of Giardini's preparatory drawings. The Berlin drawings thus form the basis of knowledge of Giardini's draughtsmanship. However, our drawing does not conform to the style exhibited in them. Some of the other drawings in the vellum album were also called Giardini (Portsmouth, 1969, nos. 96, 98), but not only does it appear that they are not by Giardini but there are such differences among the drawings that the argument that they are all by the same hand is not convincing. The attribution to Giardini is, however, understandable since the strong, late baroque forms employed here are similar to those associated with his work. They reveal Giardini's pervasive influence on Roman metalwork of the beginning of the eighteenth century.

Two other drawings by this same artist are known. One, a design for a candlestick from the same album as ours, is in the Kaufman collection (SK 92B), and the other, a half design for a *carta gloria,* is in the Cooper-Hewitt Museum (acc. no. 1938–88–2901).

ROMAN
(About 1790)

84 Design for painted ceiling decoration

Pen, black ink, colored wash, blue gouache, heightened with white. 8⁵⁄₁₆ x 6¹¹⁄₁₆ in. (211 x 170 mm). A Gothic A stamped in purple ink at lower left corner

PROVENANCE: Janos Scholz, New York
The Elisha Whittelsey Collection, The Elisha Whittelsey Fund, 52.570.36

This splendid neoclassic decoration, drawn with great delicacy and refinement, is surely by an artist, not merely a craftsman. The trompe-l'œil draperies recall Pompeii, as does the medallion with Cupid flexing his bow beside a burning tripod. The Pompeiian motifs point to a Roman origin, as does the contrast to the work of contemporary North Italians: this style is worlds away from the heavy, "archaeological" neoclassicism of Albertolli, the dashing bravura of Giani, or the luminous Venetian shimmer of Bison.

APPENDIX

Notes on the Juvarra Album (No. 36)

WATERMARKS: six-pointed star within a circle surmounted by a cross with an *F* below, near Heawood 3874; anchor within a circle surmounted by a six-pointed star with an *F* below, near Heawood 5 and 6 but lacking the letters within the circle; these first two appear most frequently; fleur-de-lys within a circle with an *F* below; fleur-de-lys in double circle surmounted by small crown; small oval escutcheon containing two monticules (?) surmounted by a flower (?), above crossed keys (?); escutcheon with cross surmounted by small crown above two vertical circles, the top one containing two nearly indecipherable letters, *ET* (?), near Heawood series 730–775, but not conforming exactly to any; bird; bird and letter *N* within a circle; three monticules surmounted by a bird within a circle surmounted by an *F*, near Heawood 166; circle containing a bird above three monticules, surmounted by a cross within a semicircle (?).

Flyleaves of rough oatmeal paper, each watermarked with an anchor within a circle surmounted by a six-pointed star with an *F* below.

COMMENTS ON SOME OF THE DRAWINGS: Juvarra's study of sixteenth-century architecture is shown, for example, in our drawings of the cornice with a detail of a bracket in the Palazzo Farnese courtyard (p. 129), the first story (p. 131), and a plan of the dado (p. 133). On p. 134, which is the verso of p. 133, is a ground plan of part of Michelangelo's Palazzo de' Conservatori on the Campidoglio, and on pages 135 and 136 are studies of his Porta Pia. Juvarra drew the capitals of the columns on the Palazzo de' Conservatori (p. 151; another study of which is on one of the small sheets pasted to leaf 3 in the volume Riserva 59–4 in the Biblioteca Nazionale, Turin). Juvarra also studied the masters of the seventeenth century, drawing Bernini's Triton Fountain (p. 59), S. Tomaso di Villanova at Castel Gandolfo (the high altar, p. 12; the interior with decoration, p. 20; and the cupola, p. 21), and S. Andrea al Quirinale (ground plan, p. 169; part of the portal of the façade, p. 171; and the interior, p. 172). Juvarra

drew many of the coats of arms that adorned Bernini's buildings throughout Rome, as well as those by other architects; many were later engraved (see Nos. 36i, j).

On the same sheet with Bernini's façade of S. Andrea (p. 171) Juvarra drew Borromini's windows on the garden façade of the Palazzo Barberini. On the verso of the ground plan of S. Andrea is Borromini's window on the main façade of the Barberini palace (p. 170). The two leaves composing these pages have been folded horizontally and the drawings are contained separately within the folded sections of the pages, as if Juvarra had folded them up to go out sketching. The buildings are situated close to one another and the drawings were probably made on the same outing. Juvarra also made studies of Borromini's work in the Lateran, drawing the frieze and cornice of the nave (p. 89), a window and capital (p. 92), a doorway (p. 161), and a doorway of Borromini's Palazzo Falconieri as well (p. 183).

Juvarra's study of Borromini is more fully documented in our album than in any other. The most interesting drawing connected with Borromini represents a section of Borromini's cupola for S. Andrea delle Fratte (p. 175); it is inscribed *disegno della cupola di S. Andrea di Fratti opera del. Sig. Cav. Borromino ño havendosi affetuata per la morte del medesimo.* Borromini's drawing for the plan of the cupola is in the Albertina, Vienna (E. Hempel, *Francesco Borromini,* Vienna, 1924, p. 168, fig. 61). It is possible that Juvarra's drawing records a lost study by Borromini for the completion of the cupola, but it is more likely his own solution for the work, which was left unfinished at Borromini's death.

Juvarra's avid search in the architecture around him for ideas is evident in a free and inventive mixture of architectural forms, combining classical and baroque motifs (p. 15). The half-attached columns at right, the bottom section plain and the top fluted, recall antiquity, as does Juvarra's play on the motif of the Colosseum seen in the background. In front of the Colosseum is a curved half colonnade with a raised pediment motif capped by an elliptical C-scroll surmounting the center of the architrave. This architectural ensemble, Hellmut Hager has suggested to me, recalls Giovanni Antonio Rossi's altar in the Cappella Lancellotti in the Lateran.

Juvarra's debt to his teacher, Carlo Fontana, appears throughout the album. A design for an altar (p. 17) is dependent on Fontana's altar in S. Teodoro al Palatino, Hager noted, which Fontana restored in 1702–04 (Fontana's drawing for the altar is in the Royal Library, Windsor Castle, and will be published in the forthcoming catalogue by A. Braham and H. Hager). In the Fontana altar, angels flank the upper portion of the altar panel, which is surmounted by a plain, triangular pediment with angels suspended from volutelike forms. In his design, Juvarra shifted the angels downward and curved the pediment. The pediment, however, also probably depends on Fontana, as it is close to details in drawings by Juvarra's pupil Bernardo Vittone after projects of Fontana (on the Vittone drawings, see R. Wittkower, "Vittone's drawings in the Musée des Arts Décoratifs, Paris," *Studies in Renaissance and Baroque Art presented to Anthony Blunt on his 60th birthday,* London and New York, 1967, pp. 165–172).

A chapel wall with two doors united by a concave, curved pediment below an arched picture frame (p. 106) is a direct copy, in which Juvarra even indicated measurements, of the Cappella Montioni in S. Maria in Montesanto, built by Tommaso Mattei but dependent on a design by Fontana, as was also pointed out to me by Hager. Vittone was equally interested in the motif and drew it (see Wittkower, "Vittone's drawings," p. 171, pl. XXX, fig. 12). Juvarra also drew a cartouche of a coat of arms inscribed *Cav. Carlo Fontana* (p. 4 of our album), probably a study of a coat of arms designed by Fontana that embellished one of his buildings. Juvarra may have considered using it in his book of etchings, *Raccolta di varie targhe* (see Nos. 36i, j), which contains two Fontana designs.

In addition to the *targhe,* there are other projects for prints in the album, for example, a series of rosettes in black chalk on pp. 23, 25, 27, 29, 31, 33, 35, 37, and 39. Several of the succeeding pages are prepared with border outlines for more rosettes.

A detailed account of the album will be published in the forthcoming *Corpus Juvarrianum* by Henry A. Millon.

The Drawings

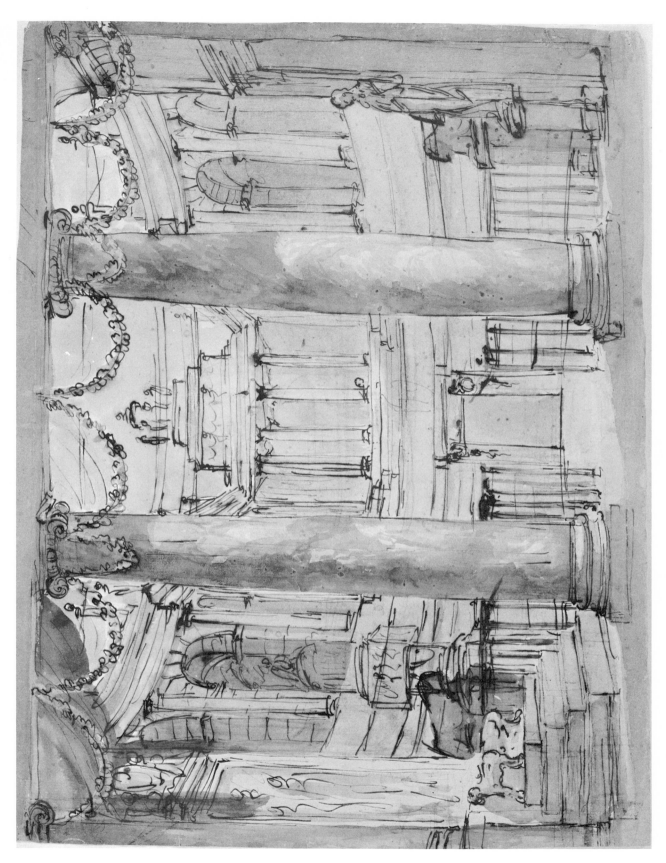

2

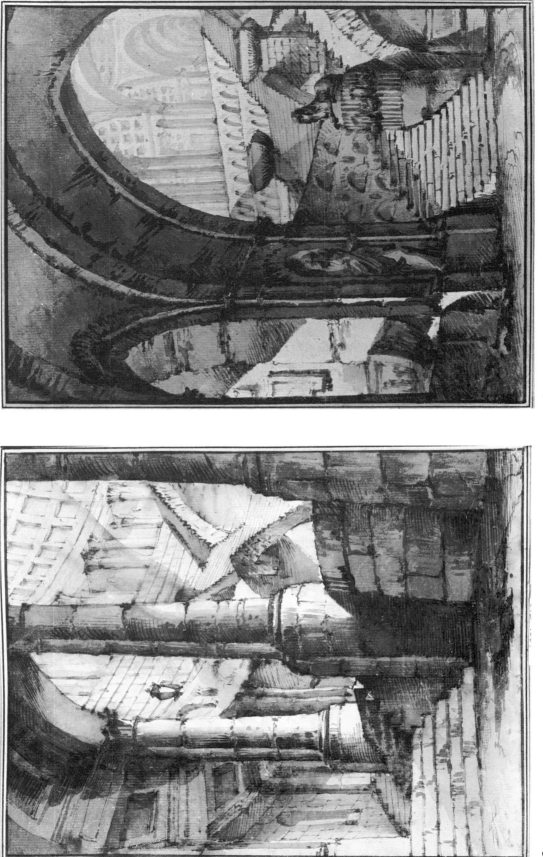

4

3

5

6

8

7

10

9

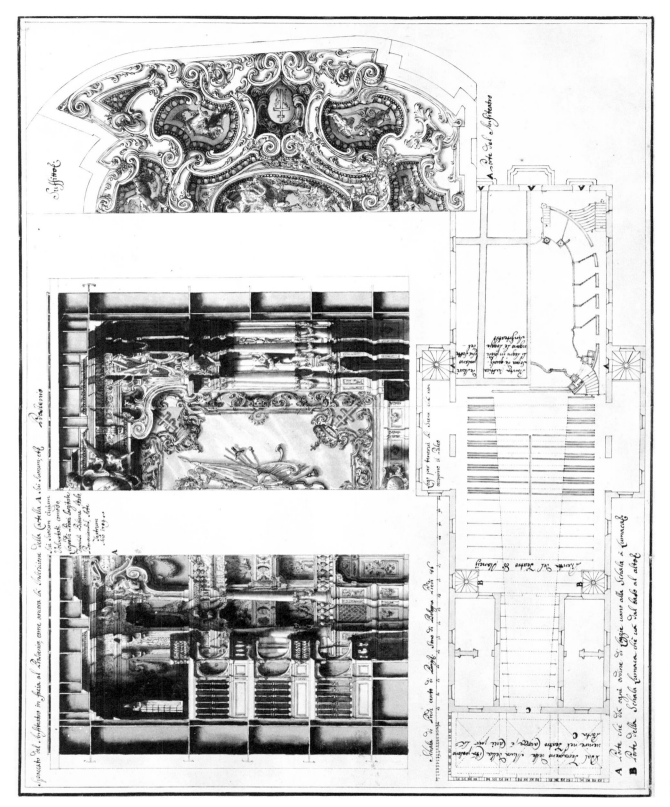

11

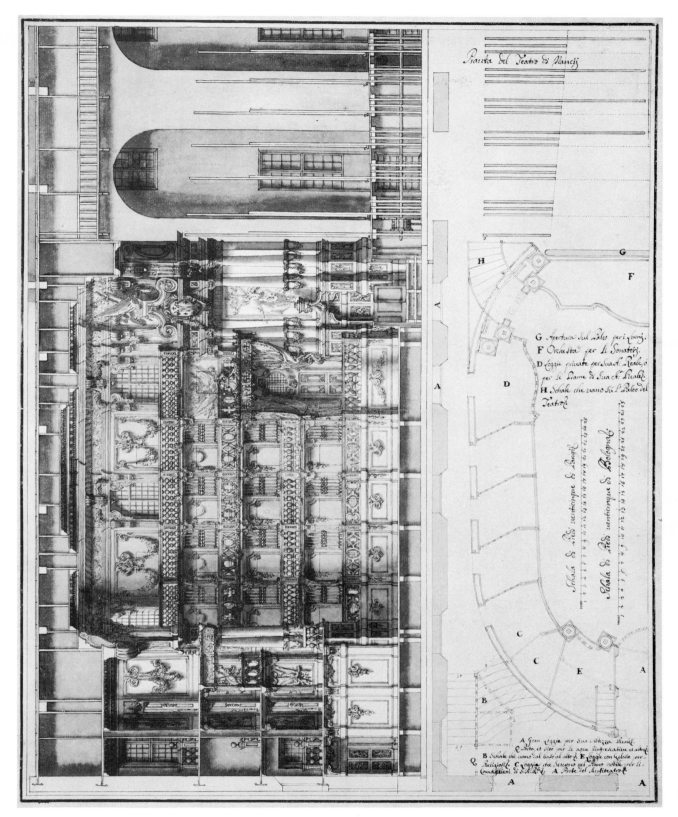

13

14

15

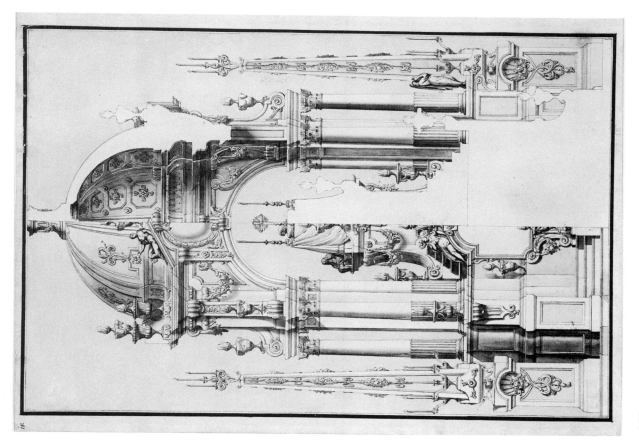

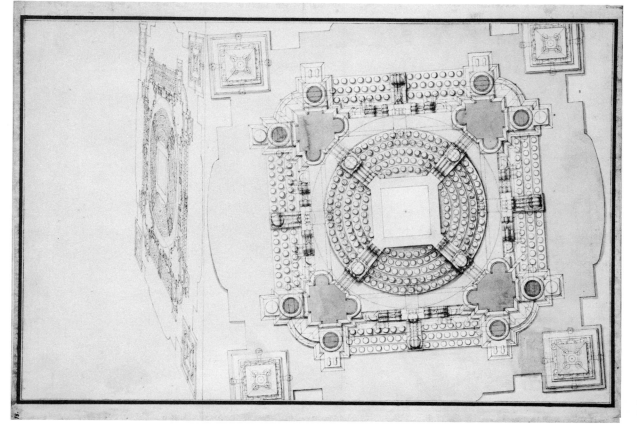

17

16

18

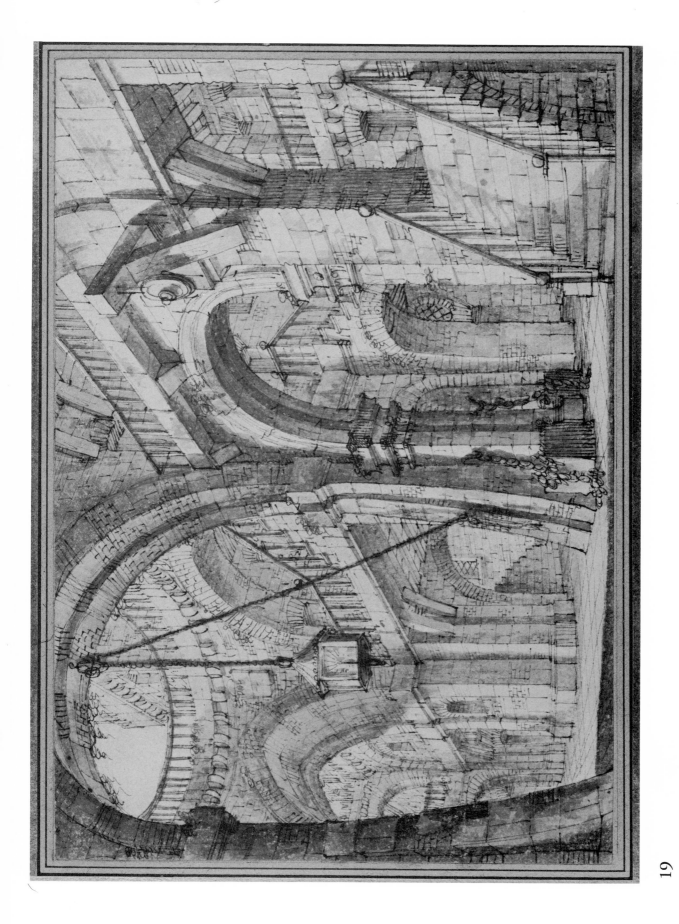

19

20

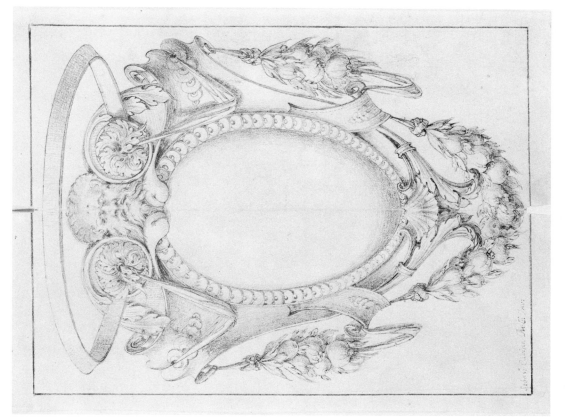

21b

21a

22

23 a   23 b

24

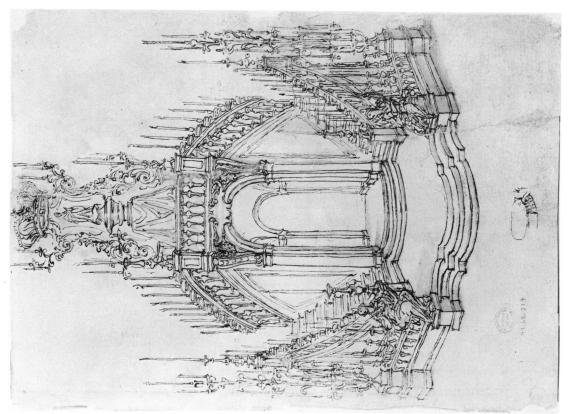

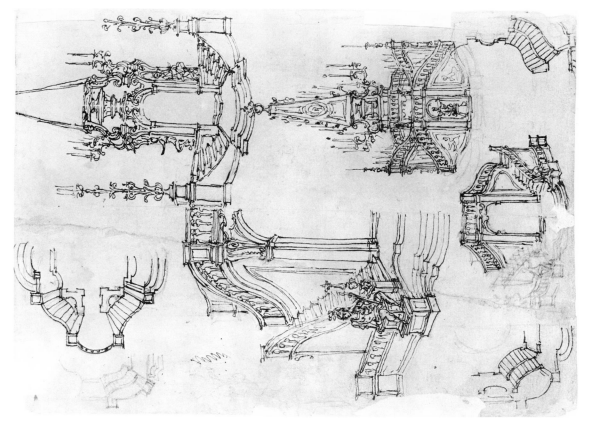

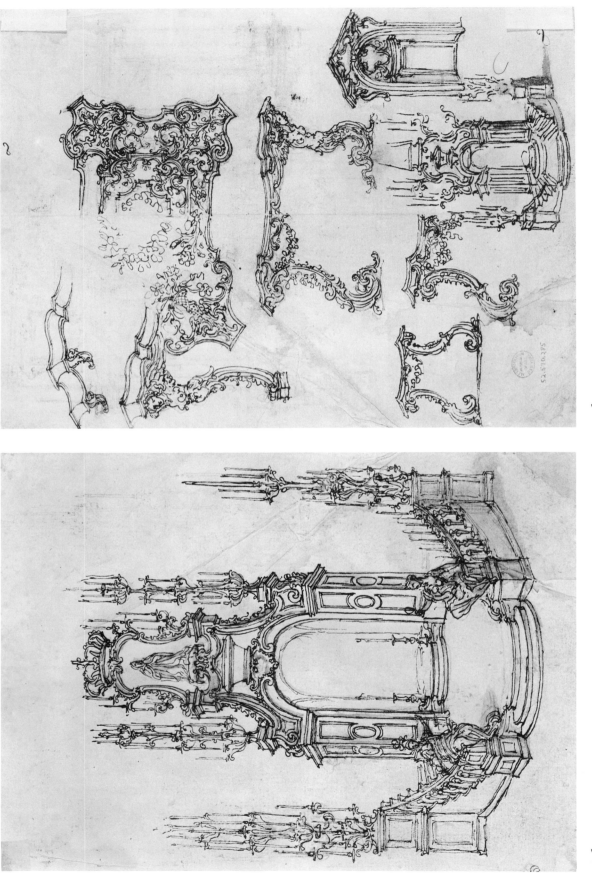

26 verso

26

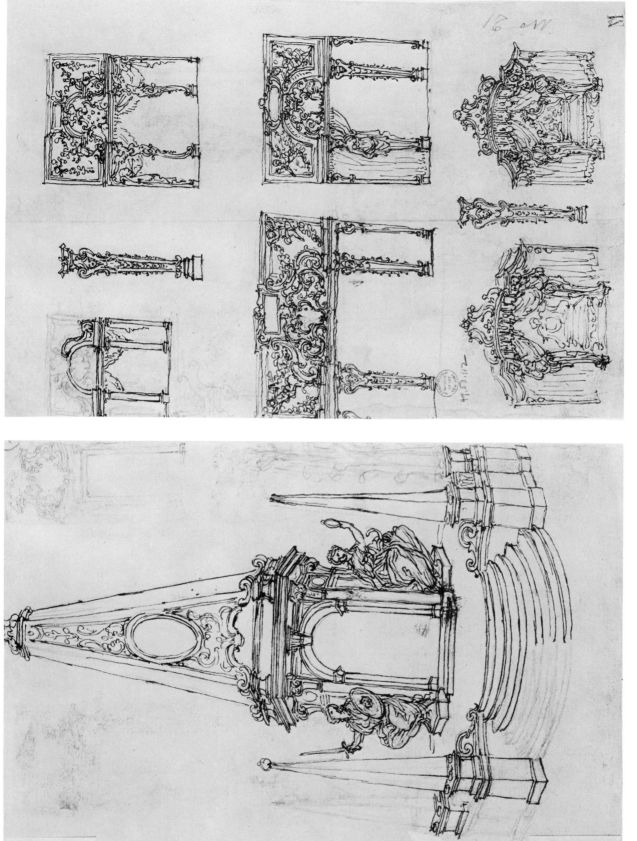

28

28 verso

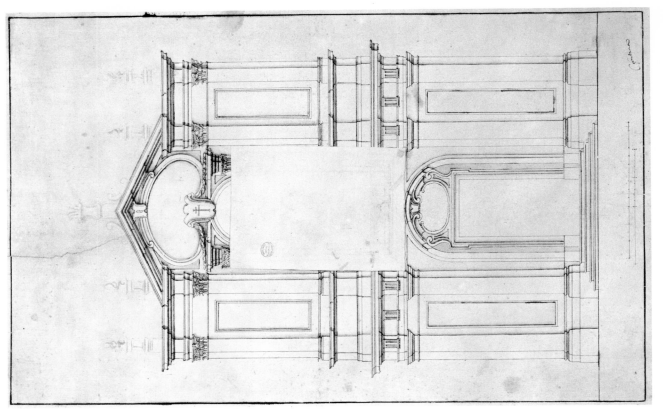

29b

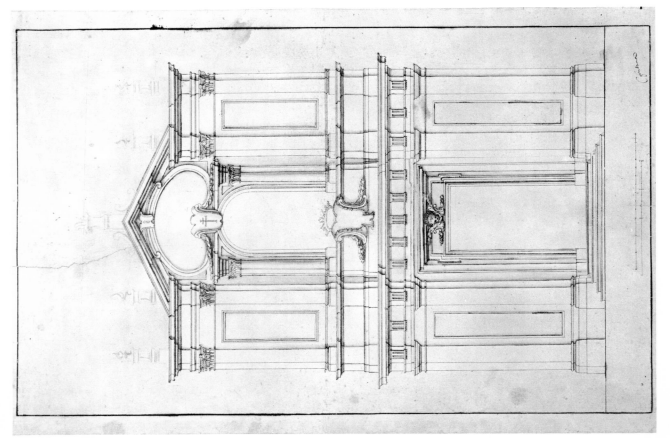

29a

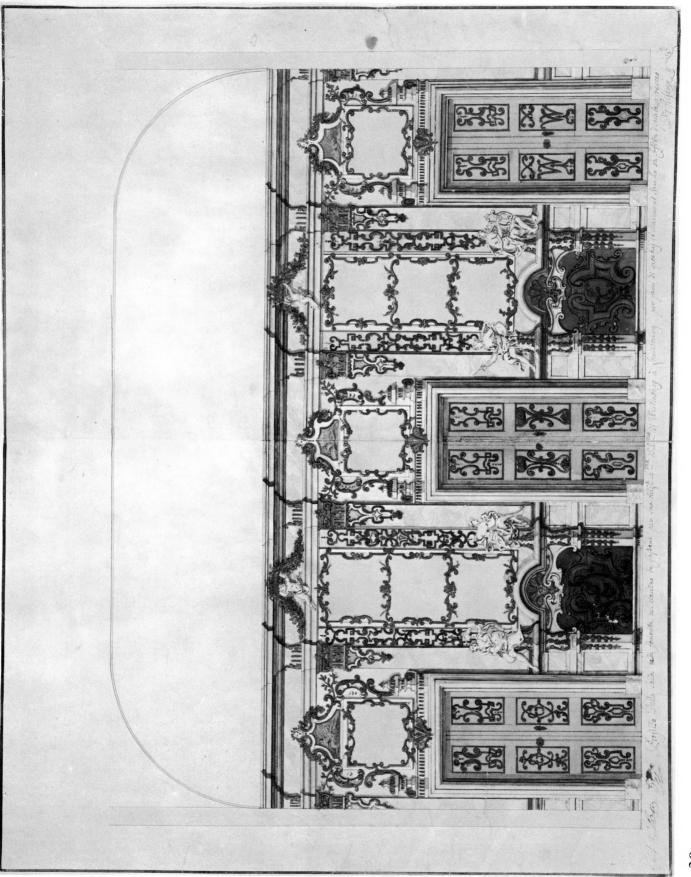

31

31 verso

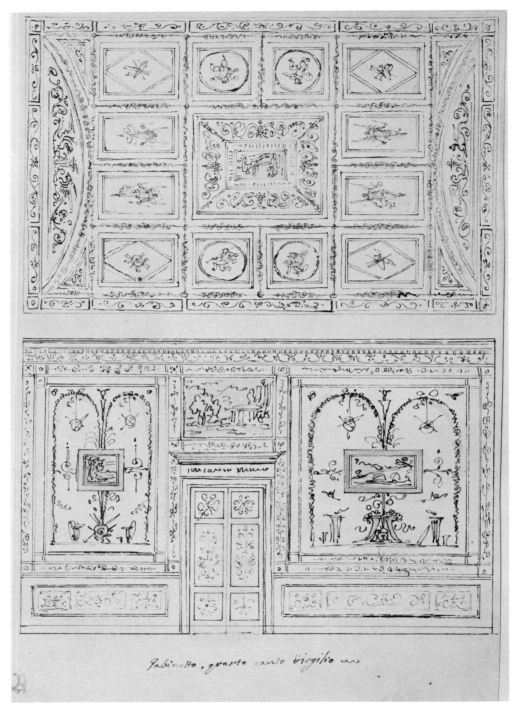

Gabinetto, quarto canto virgilio

33 a

camera da ricevere canto sesto Virgilio

33b

Trumeau sop: Camo
del Giannotti 1742

34

35

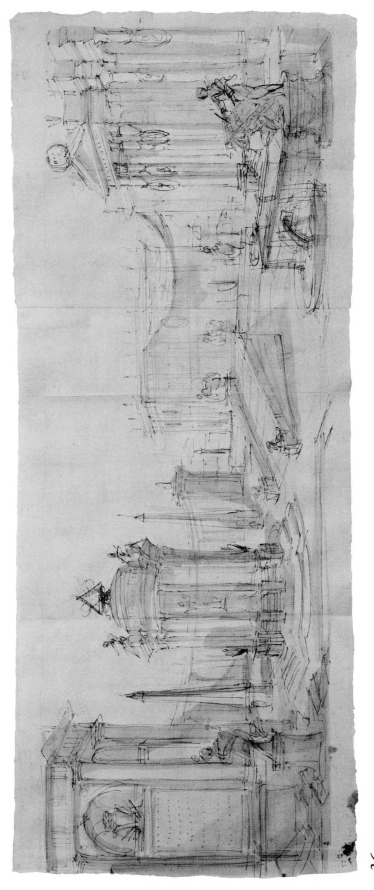

36a

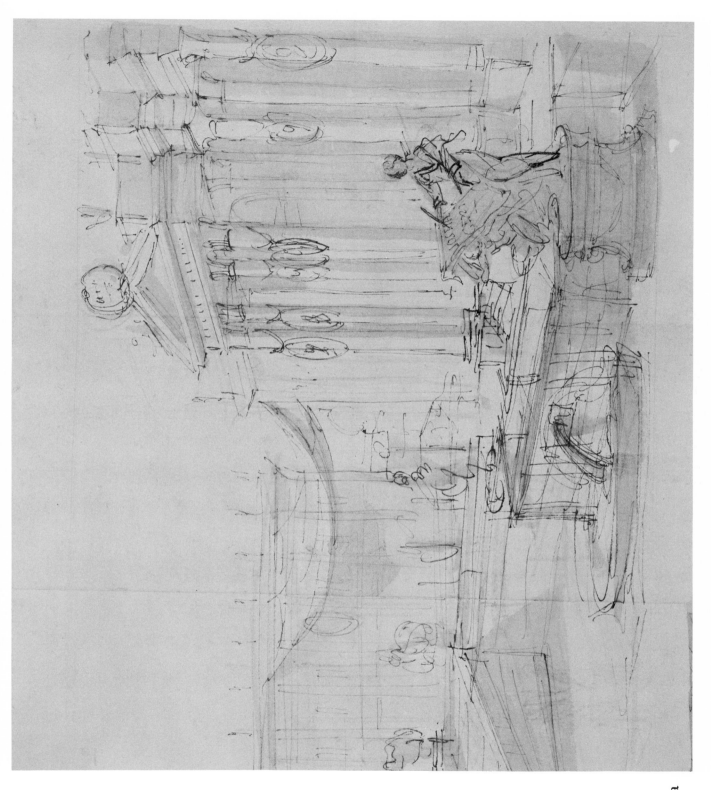

Detail of 36a

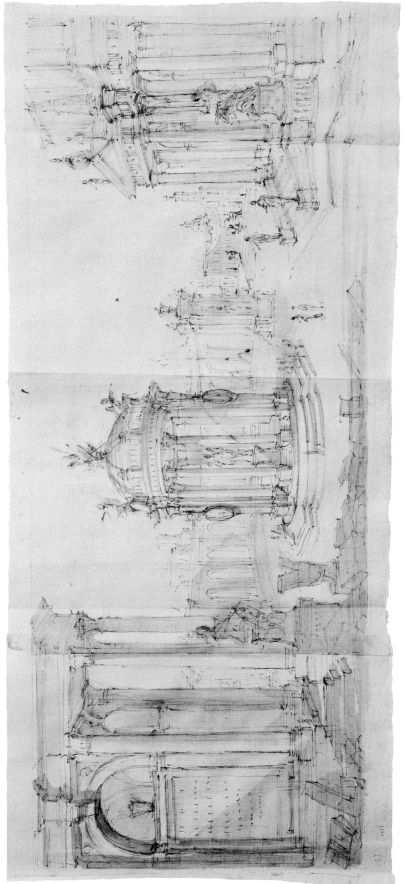

36b

Prospettive fatte a S.ti Apostoli
1704. in Roma

36c

36d

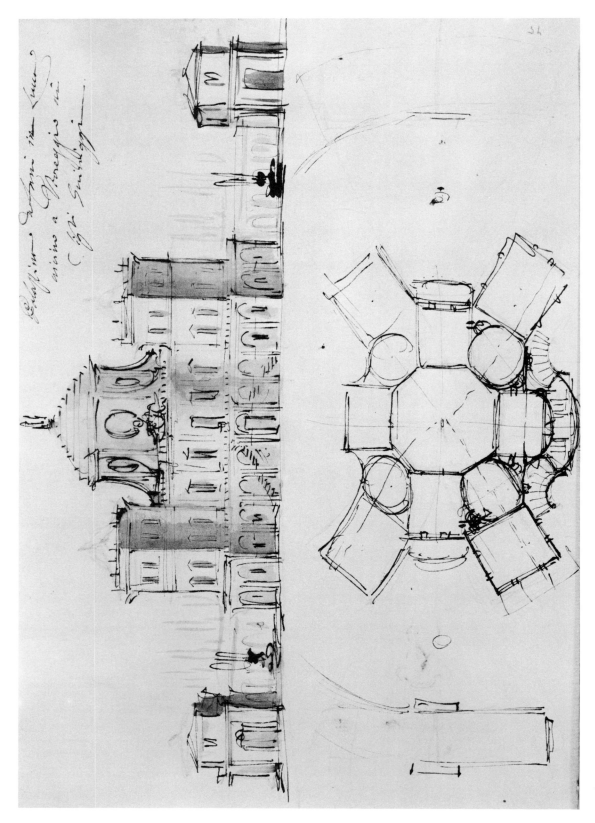

36f

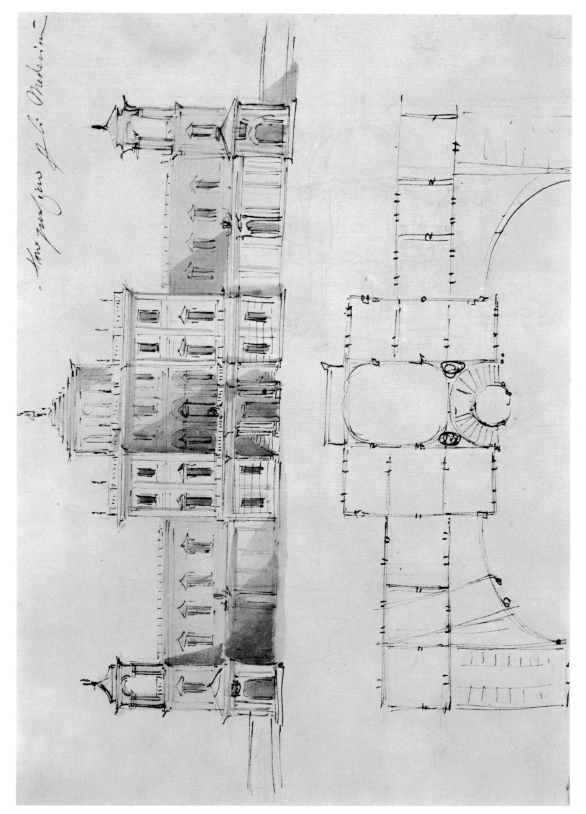

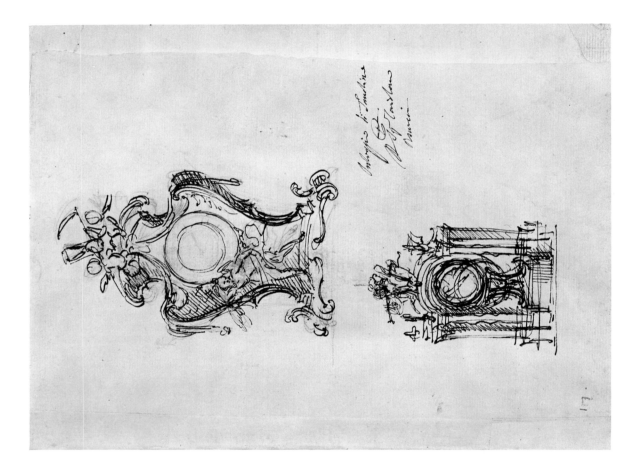

36j

36i

Primo pensiero p. la Capella di S. Filippo al Girolamo
del S.r Andrea Anesina, messa in opera l'anno 1707

235

36k

Secondo pensiero
della Capella d'Alpr.
in S. Giuliano.

249

361

Cappella Antamoro, S. Girolamo della Carità, Rome (Photo: Phyllis Dearborn Massar)

Drawing Room

37

38

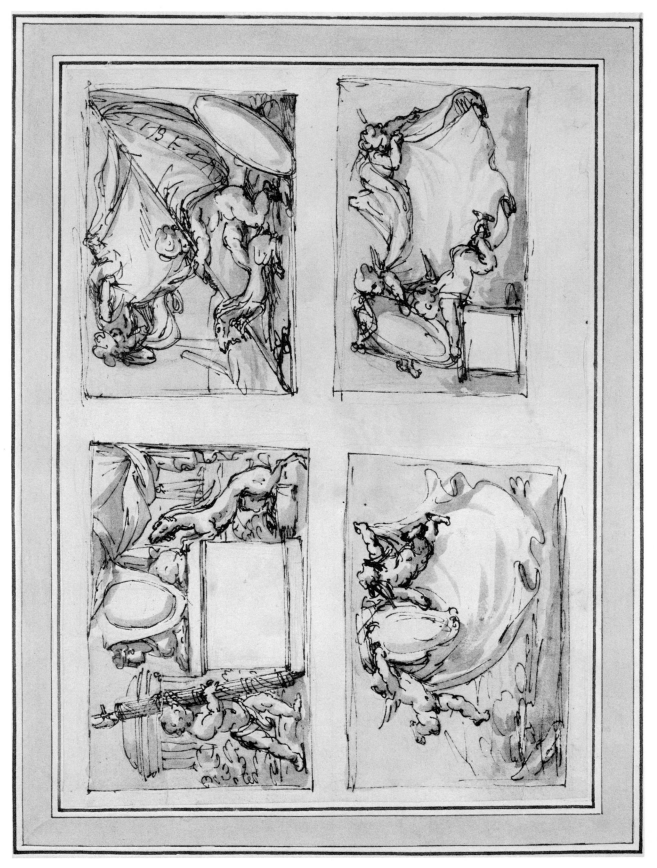

39

40

Disegno approvato per il ornamento della Camera di S. Perone di V.A.R. il dis[?] Francesco di Parma [...]
[...] a[...] 1778   Borellino a[...]

41

42

43

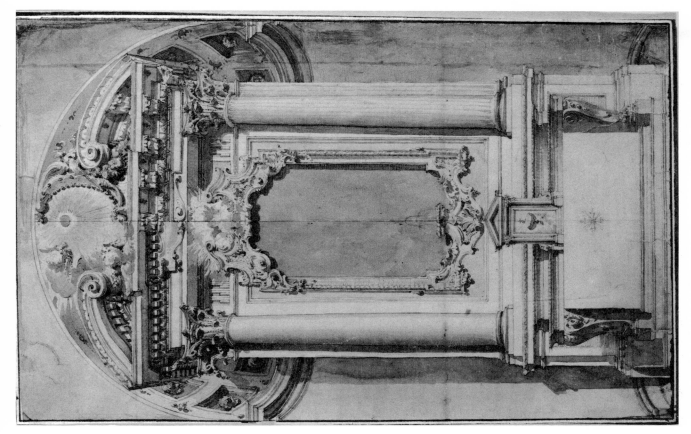

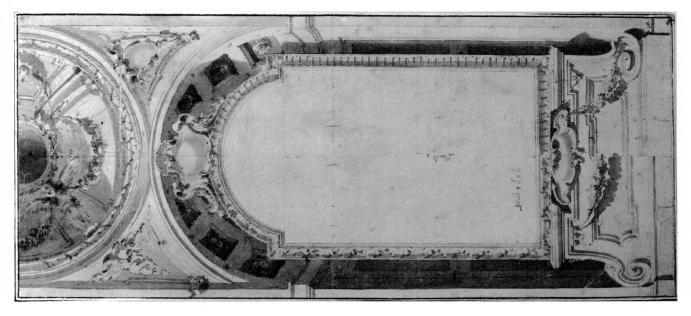

44b

44a

45

46

oncie 18.   oncie 9.   o. 9.   o. 9.

1   2   3   4

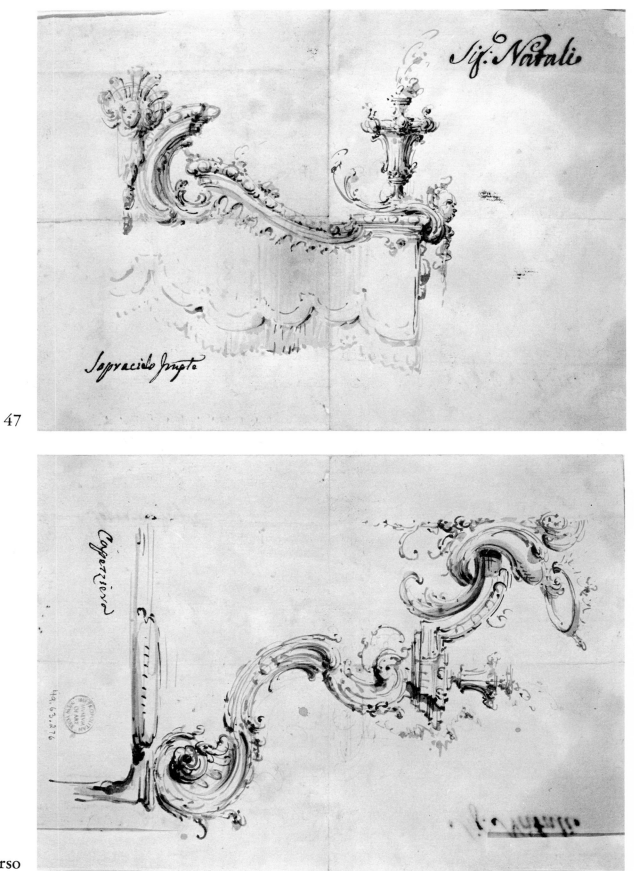

47

47 verso

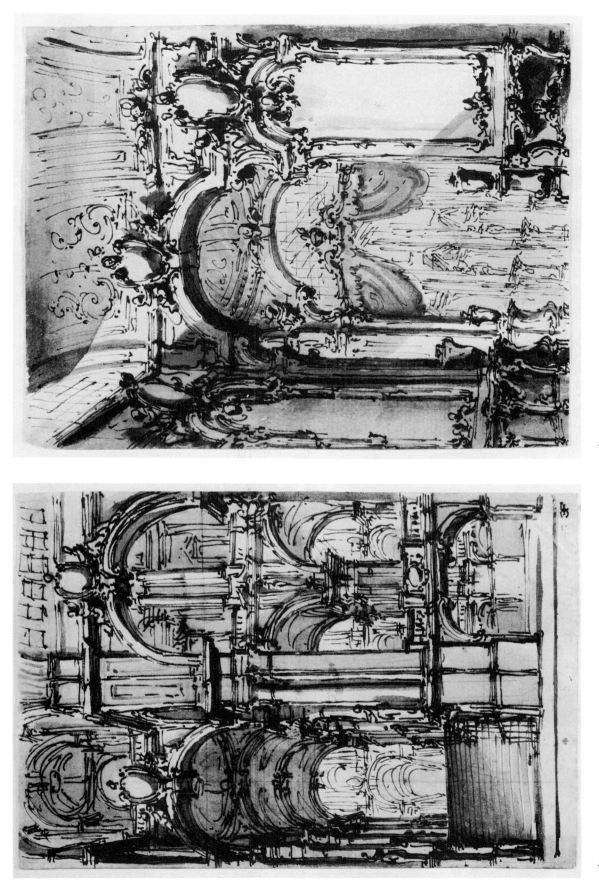

49

48

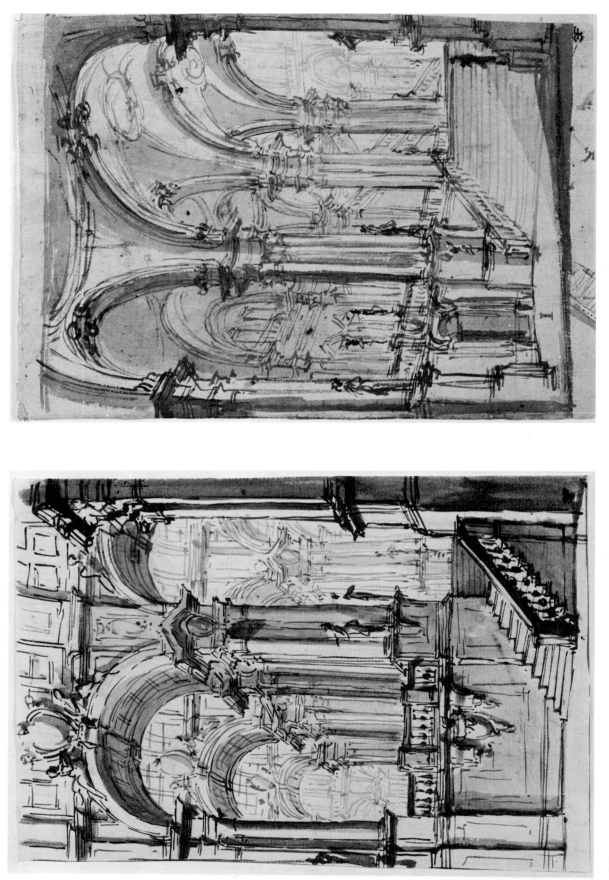

50a

50b

51 verso

51

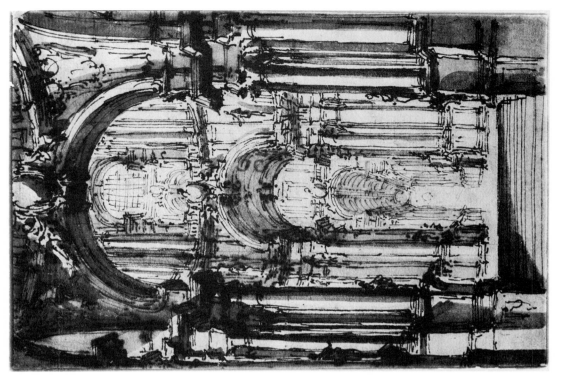

52b

52a

Vincenzo Rè Inventore, e delineatore.

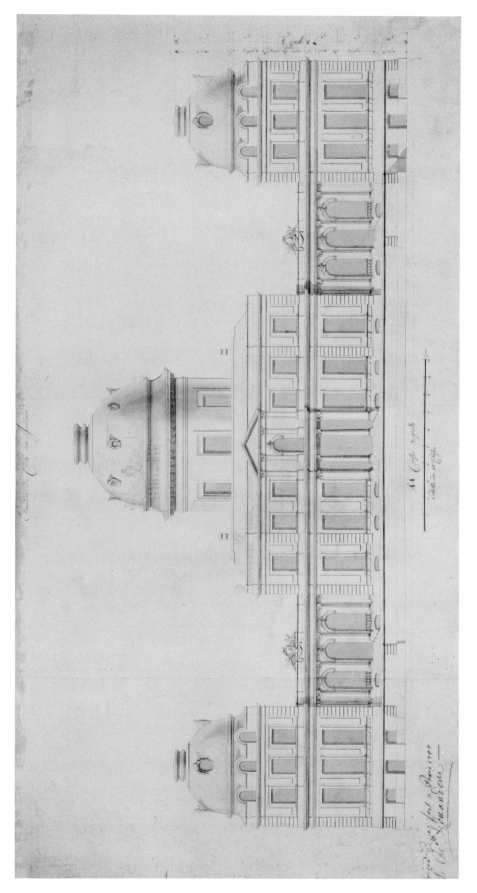

56

57

58

59

Cappella delle Reliquie
di S. Ciriaco d'Ancona

61

62

63

64

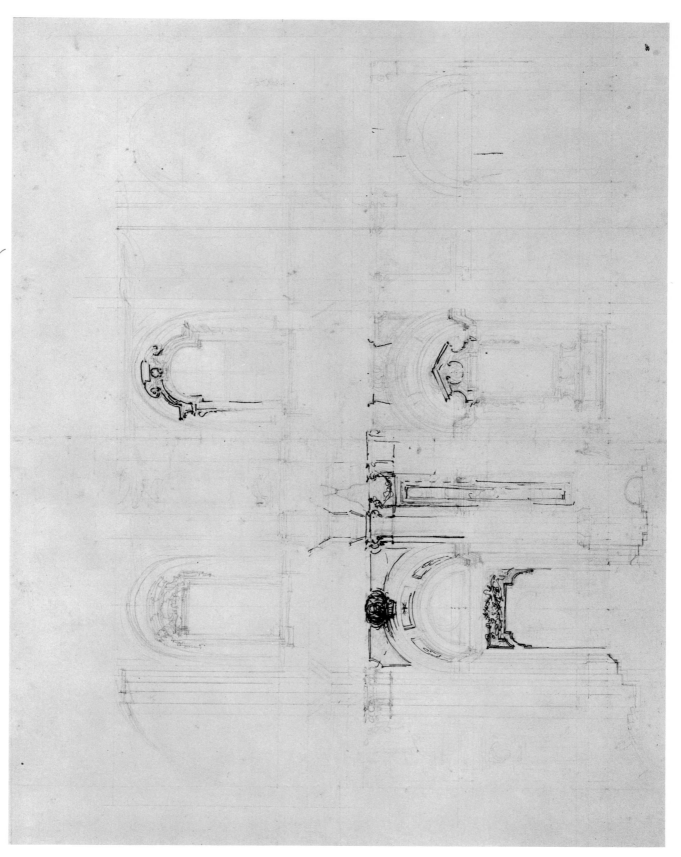

65

66

67

67 verso

68

68 verso

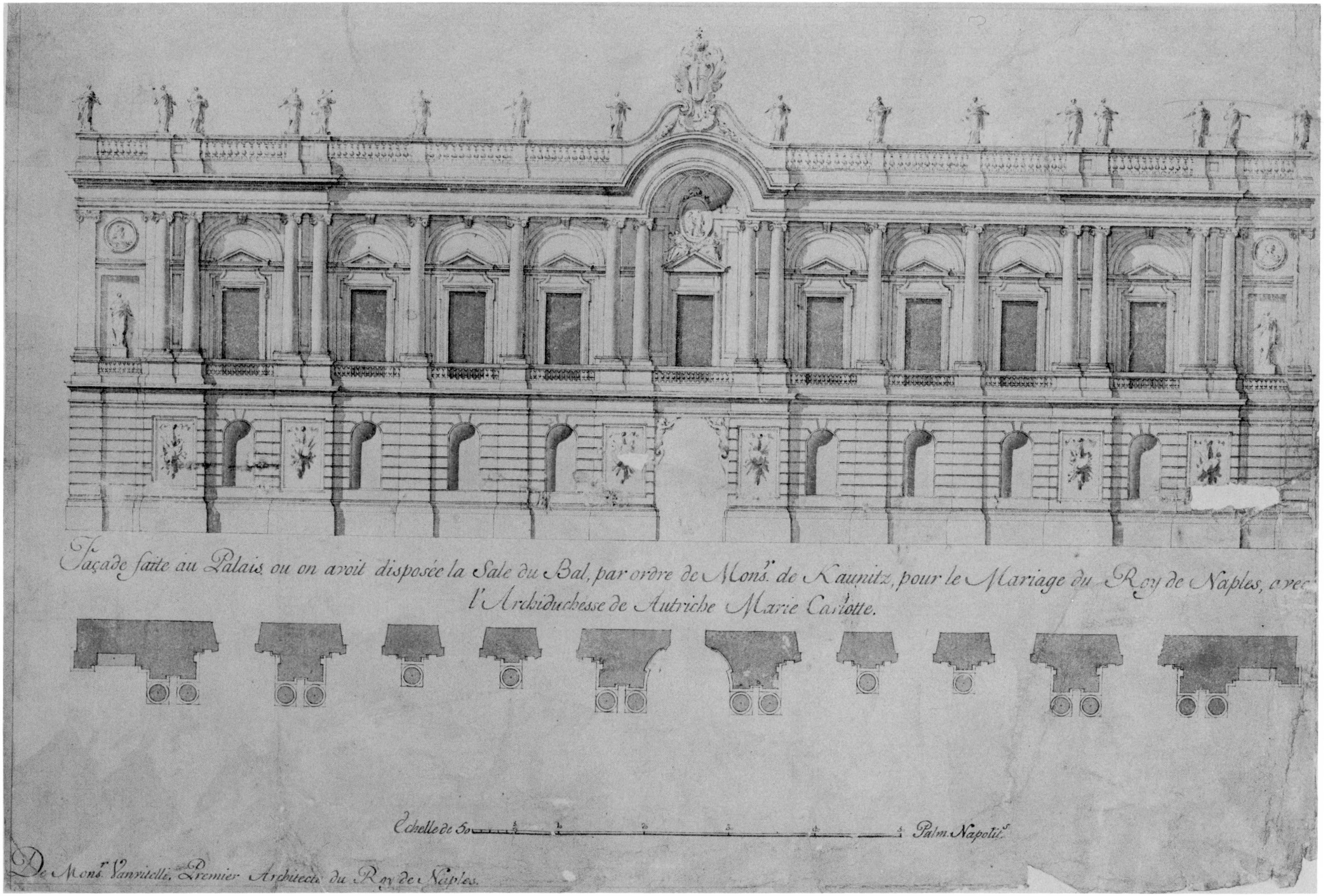

Façade faite au Palais ou on avoit disposée la Sale du Bal, par ordre de Mons.r de Kaunitz, pour le Marriage du Roy de Naples, avec l'Archiduchesse de Autriche Marie Carlotte.

Echelle de 30

Palmi Napoli.

Mons.r Vanvitelli, Premier Architecte du Roy de Naples.

69

Coupe sur la Longueur de la Salle du Bal, disposée par ordre de Monsr de Kaunitz, pour le Mariage du Roy de Naples, avec
l'Archiduchesse de Autriche Marie Carlotte

Echelle de 50 _____ 4 Palm. Napolit.^f

De Monsr V.^{le} Vanvitelli. C.^B P.^{er} Architecte du Roy de Naples.

70

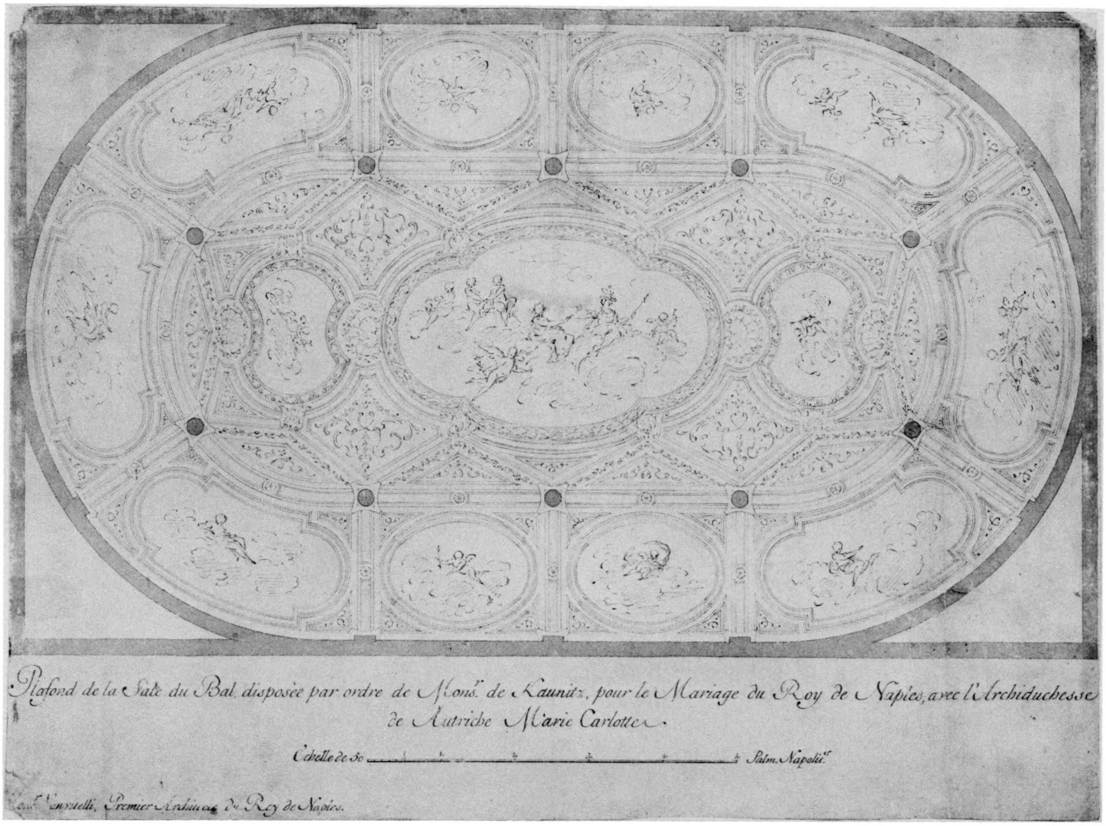

Plafond de la Sale du Bal, disposée par ordre de Mons. de Kaunitz, pour le Mariage du Roy de Naples, avec l'Archiduchesse de Autriche Marie Carlotte.

Echelle de 50 ⸺⸺⸺⸺ Palm. Napolit.

par L. Vanvitelli, Premier Architecte du Roy de Naples.

71

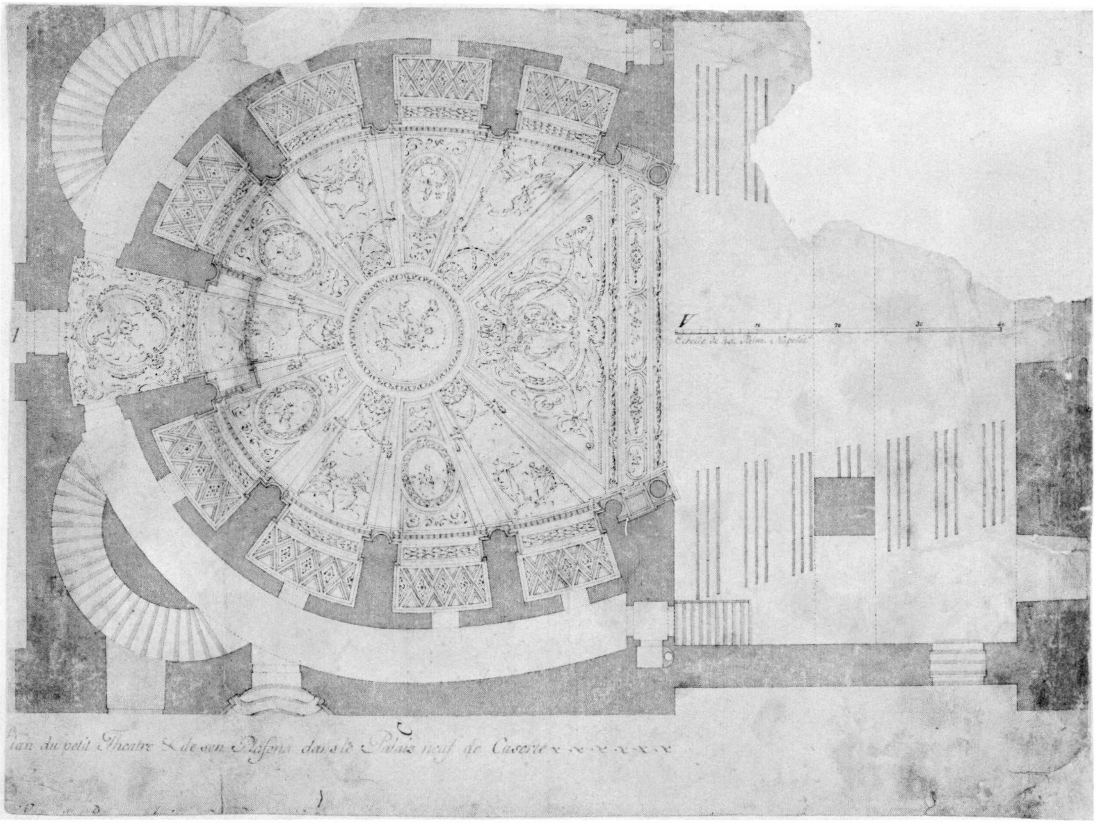

Plan du petit Theatre & de son Plafond dans le Palais neuf de Caserte ⸺⸺⸺

Echelle de Palm. Napolit.

72

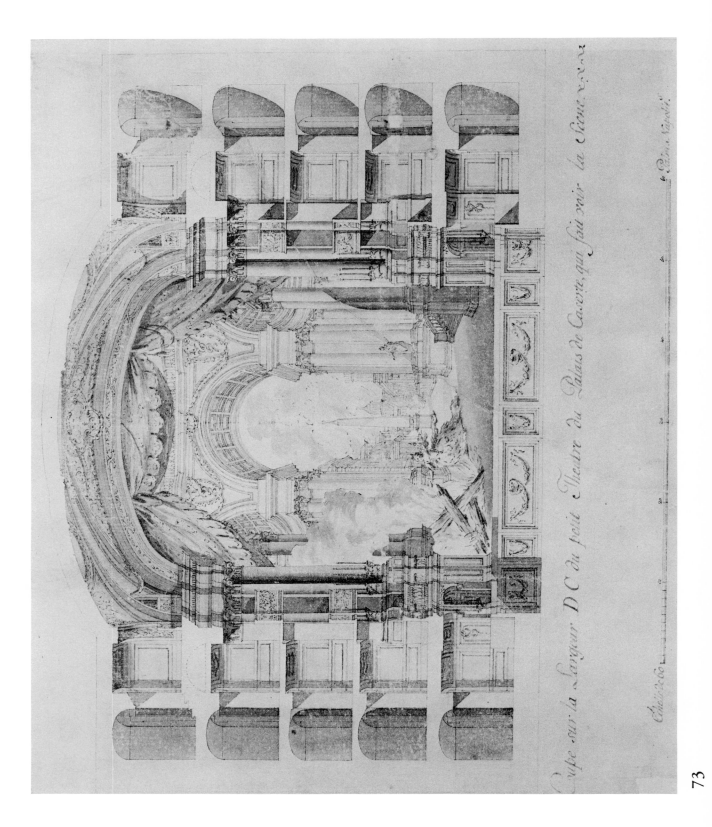

Coupe sur la Largeur D C du petit Theatre du Palais de Cautere, qui fait voir la Scene *****

Echelle de 60   6. Perche Napole.

73

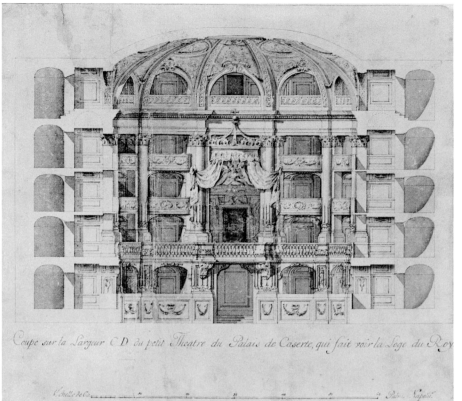

Coupe sur la Largeur C D du petit Theatre du Palais de Caserte, qui fait voir la Loge du Roy

Echelle de 60   10   20   30   40   50   P. Palm. Napolit.

74

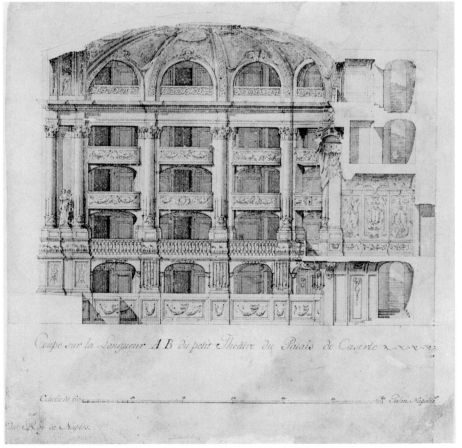

Coupe sur la Longueur A B du petit Theatre du Palais de Caserte

Echelle de 60   10   20   30   40   50   P. Palm. Napolit.

du Roy de Naples.

75

gran. Salla. Darme.

77a

77b

77c

78

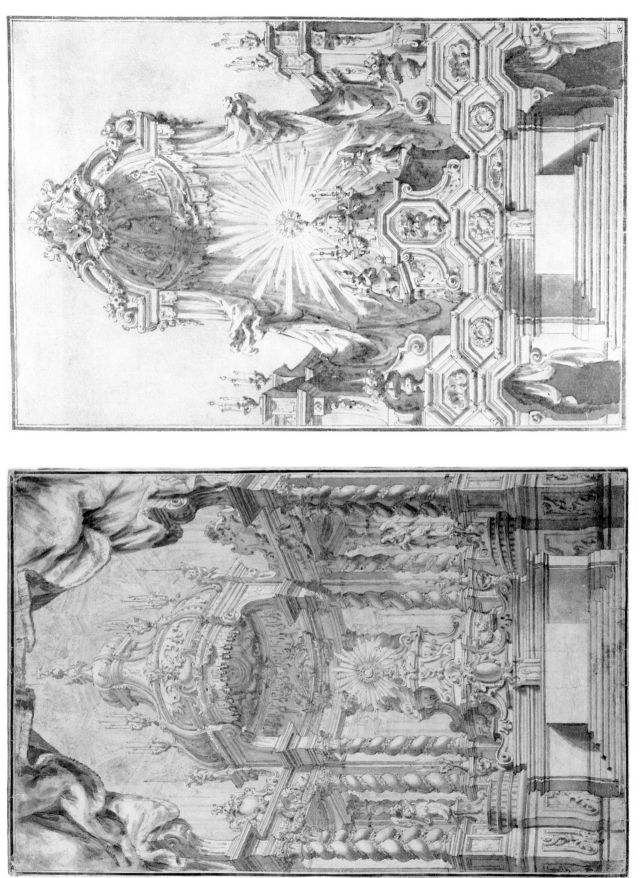

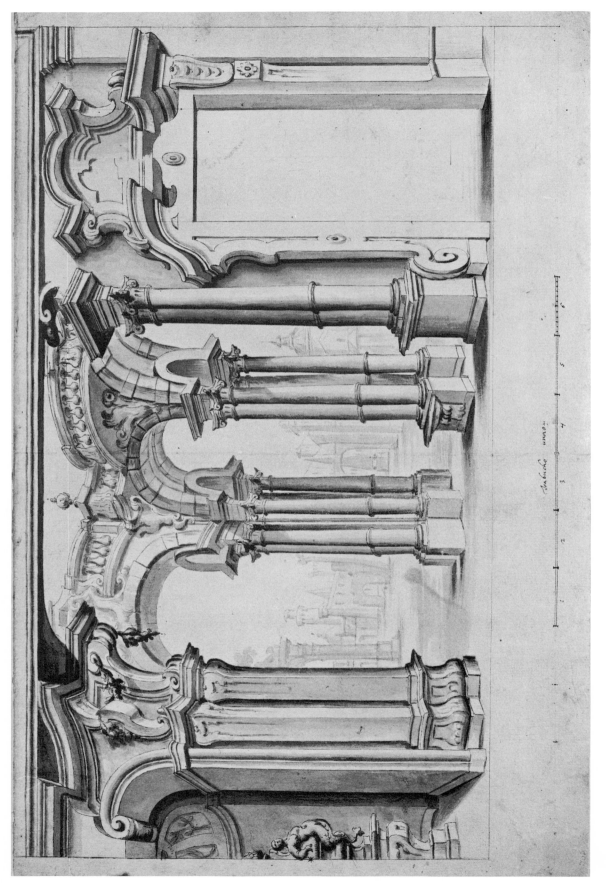

82

83

84

Drawing of an escutcheon with the Medici arms
(see catalogue entry 27)